Here's How

Apply to American Colleges and Universities

Maya Brennan
Sarah Briggs

NTC LearningWorks

NTC/Contemporary Publishing Company

Library of Congress Cataloging-in-Publication Data

Brennan, Moya.
    [How to apply to American colleges and universities]
    Apply to American colleges and universities / Moya Brennan
and Sarah Briggs.
       p.   cm.—(Here's how)
    Previously published as: How to apply to American colleges and
universities. © 1992.
    Includes index.
    ISBN 0-8442-2479-0
    1. College applications—United States—Handbooks, manuals,
etc. I. Briggs, Sarah L. (Sarah Lee) , 1942–   . II. Title.
III. Series: Here's how (Lincolnwood, Ill.)
  [LB2351.46.B74   1998]
  378.1'056—DC21   97-49442

To Jelly Roll

Cover illustrations by Art Glazer

Published by NTC LearningWorks
An imprint of NTC/Contemporary Publishing Company
4255 West Touhy Avenue, Lincolnwood (Chicago), Illinois 60646-1975 U.S.A.
Copyright © 1998 by NTC/Contemporary Publishing Company
Printed in the United States of America
International Standard Book Number: 0-8442-2479-0
 18   17   16   15   14   13   12   11   10   9   8   7   6   5   4   3   2   1

Contents

Preface   **v**
    To the Student
    To the ESL Instructor
    To the Educational Advisor
    Acknowledgments

About the Authors   **ix**

1 I Want to Study in the United States. What Do I Do?   **1**
    Applying for Undergraduate Study in the United States   2
    Applying for Graduate Study in the United States   5
    Understanding the Application Process   7

2 How Do I Get Application and Program Information?   **13**
    Choosing Universities to Write To   14
    Writing to University Admissions Offices   17
    Getting Information about Graduate Programs   23
    Evaluating Graduate Programs   27

3 What Tests Do I Need to Take?   **31**
    General Testing Information   32
    English Language Tests   38
    Undergraduate Applicants—Academic Tests   45
    Graduate Applicants—Academic Tests and Special English Tests   52

4 What Are These Application Instructions and Forms Telling Me?   **57**
    Application Instructions and Forms   58
    Graduate Applications   60
    Areas of Study   62
    Begin at the Beginning, But...   62

5 How Do I Complete the Application Form?   **69**
  Giving Personal Data   70
  Applying for a Course of Study   73
  Defining Your Race   75
  Describing Your English Language Skills   77
  What I Learned in School   79
  Describing Your Employment Experience   81

6 What Writing Do I Need to Do?   **87**
  Understanding What to Write in the Personal Statement   88
  Writing the Personal Statement   91
  Revising the Personal Statement   93
  Writing a Statement of Purpose   96

7 How Do I Pay for My Studies?   **99**
  What Financial Assistance Is Available?   100
  Financial Assistance from the University for Graduate Students 104
  Providing Financial Certification   106

8 What Else Must Be Completed to Apply?   **113**
  Building a Complete Application   114
  Giving Proof of Your Educational Background   116
  Arranging for References/Letters of Recommendation   121
  Understanding the Visa Process   124
  Finishing Up   127

9 Follow-up Correspondence   **131**
  Did I Forget to Send Something?   132
  Did I Get In?   133
  Writing Letters of Acceptance and Refusal   136

Appendixes   **139**
  1 Names in the United States   140
  2 Undergraduate Applicants to Community Colleges   141
  3 U.S. Universities with the Most International Students   142
  4 Sample Graduate Application for Admission   144
  5 Answers to Exercises   147

Credits and Acknowledgments   **157**

Index   **159**

Preface

TO THE STUDENT

In our many years of teaching English, we have often been asked to help students with their applications to U.S. colleges and universities. We wrote *How to Apply to American Colleges and Universities* to address this need for information and advice about the application process.

This manual provides you with the *basic information* and *skills* you need to apply successfully to a U.S. college or university, at the undergraduate or graduate level. It is based on our experiences and the advice of U.S. college and university admissions officers and international students already in the United States.

Each chapter helps you complete your applications effectively by providing you with:

- The essential information you need to understand every step of the application process.
- Sample application forms and practice exercises to help you prepare to complete your applications.
- Question and answer sections that provide valuable advice for improving your applications along with descriptions of common problems to avoid.

You probably already know that information brochures, catalogs, and application forms can be difficult to read. However, as you work with the many examples from authentic university applications provided in this book, you will improve your reading and writing skills and the task of applying to study in the United States will become easier.

You will understand the process not only from the student's point of view, but also from the admissions officer's point of view. This will give you invaluable help in submitting an application that has been correctly and intelligently completed. You will have a better chance of admission to the college or university of your choice.

We wish you success in completing your applications and with your studies in the United States.

TO THE ESL INSTRUCTOR

This complete manual enables students to develop a schema of the U.S. educational system and of the college and university application process within it. For domestic applicants, completing an application can be difficult and time consuming. It is even more so for the international applicant who may not have the cultural background and easy access to print and personal sources that can help build the body of knowledge and language skills necessary to efficiently and correctly complete the application.

Moreover, for the international student the application process itself varies in some ways from the process for domestic students, so ESL instructors from the United States often find it difficult to draw on their own experiences in advising domestic applicants. ESL instructors from the United States and internationally will find this manual an excellent resource for use in familiarizing themselves with every aspect of the international student application process, and in advising international applicants.

While *How to Apply to American Colleges and Universities* offers material that is particularly relevant to international students, it is designed to help *all* students learn independently about the university application process. It addresses them directly and uses excerpts from authentic material to facilitate their understanding of the information they will encounter when they apply to study at the undergraduate or graduate level in the United States.

This manual can also be used in courses and workshops in high schools and English language programs, both in the United States and abroad. It is ideal for high-interest, task-based courses for students whose goals include studying in the United States.

TO THE EDUCATIONAL ADVISOR

This book is designed to help students with the process of applying to a U.S. college or university. We have included information and advice that will be useful to students interested in graduate study as well as to those interested in undergraduate study.

This manual contains guidelines for meeting the academic, financial, and official requirements for studying in the United States with practice exercises based on authentic forms, documents, brochures, and catalogs. We also advise students to seek help from their counselors and advisors, teachers, friends, and fellow students. It is our hope that when students come to you for advice, they will better be able to utilize the resources that you have available for them—the books, videos, and consultation time. They will bring with them a stronger understanding of the U.S. educational system, and of what is expected of them as prospective students. In this way, the time you spend with them will be more beneficial.

ACKNOWLEDGMENTS

In order to give our readers the widest possible perspective on the application process, we have held discussions with and sent questionnaires to admissions officers from a cross section of colleges and universities throughout the United States—public and private; small, medium, and large; two-year community colleges, four-year colleges, and universities with undergraduate and graduate programs. We sincerely appreciate the thought and the time given by admissions officers, and many of their comments and advice have been included in this book.

We also appreciate the suggestions made by the many students we have talked to about the application process.

Moya Brennan
Sarah Briggs

About the Authors

MOYA BRENNAN teaches in the English Language Program, University of California, Santa Barbara Extension. She holds an MA in Applied Linguistics from the University of Lancaster, England.

SARAH BRIGGS is a researcher at the English Language Institute at the University of Michigan. She holds an MS in International Education and a Ph.D. in English Education from Indiana University.

I Want to Study in the United States. What Do I Do?

► **APPLYING FOR UNDERGRADUATE STUDY IN THE UNITED STATES**

► **APPLYING FOR GRADUATE STUDY IN THE UNITED STATES**

► **UNDERSTANDING THE APPLICATION PROCESS**

How much do you know about applying for university study in the United States? Answer these questions and find out. Write either *True* or *False* in the blank after each sentence. (Answers are given in Appendix 5 on page 147.)

1. The only way to become a student at a U.S. university is to apply to be a student. _____

2. A student's parents or a student's friend can apply for a student. _____

3. An application form and documents (academic records and other official papers) must be sent to each university that a student might like to attend. _____

4. A person can apply to only four U.S. universities in one year. _____

5. It costs money to apply to a U.S. university. _____

6. An international student can begin studies only in September. _____

7. To apply for study in the United States, a student must have between $10,000 and $25,000 for each year of U.S. study. _____

8. A student can attend one U.S. university and then change to another one without making a new application. _____

9. The application process is different for international students than it is for U.S. citizens. _____

10. The application process is different for every college or university. _____

How did you do? This book will help you to learn about and understand every step of the application process. You will be working with sections from the application forms of many universities. This will help you when you complete your application forms and build your application file for each university.

Remember, many U.S. colleges and universities want international students. The application process is complicated and confusing, but you can be successful. U.S. universities are not trying to make the procedure confusing. It is confusing because each university is different and the applicants must provide a lot of information to every university.

APPLYING FOR UNDERGRADUATE STUDY IN THE UNITED STATES

If you are considering going to the United States to study after you finish secondary school (high school), you will apply for undergraduate study. Look at Figure 1A. Most international students apply to four-year programs, but many complete a two-year program at a community college and then transfer to a four-year college or university for their last two years of study. (See Appendix 2, page 141 for information about community colleges.)

The degree a student receives from a university depends on the number of courses the student has taken and passed. Each course is worth a certain amount of credit. Read these examples:

Keiko Samu attended a U.S. community college. She took twenty courses. Each course was worth three credits. She has sixty credit hours. She received an associate's degree. Her major was hotel and restaurant management.

Marie-France Vouvray is enrolled in a liberal arts program at a university in California. Her major is history. She has taken twenty courses. She has sixty credit hours. She will not get her degree until she takes more courses. She needs 120 credits for a bachelor's degree.

Figure 1A.   The United States Educational System

Grade	Type of School	Student Age
1–6	elementary school	6–11
7–9	middle school or junior high school	12–14
10–12	high school	15–18

degree granted: high school diploma

Undergraduate Study

Year	Type of School	Student Age
freshman	community college or junior college	18 +
sophomore	college or university	19 +
junior		20 +
senior		21 +

degrees granted: associate's degree (for 2 years of study), bachelor's degree (for 4 years of study)

Graduate Study

Year	Type of School	Student Age
1–5 +	university (with a graduate school program)	21 +

degrees granted: master's degree (for 1–2 years of study), doctoral degree (for 3 or more years of study)

The first two years of undergraduate study (the freshman and sophomore years) are usually a general course of study. By the third (junior) year, students begin to specialize. A specialized professional program such as engineering may take a year longer to complete than a regular liberal arts program such as history or chemistry.

If you have done some advanced study or university coursework in your own country, but you don't have a university degree equivalent to the U.S. bachelor's degree, you must enter a U.S. university as an undergraduate student. However, you may receive some credit for the college-level work you have done. You may not have to begin at the freshman level. Read this example:

Ali has completed secondary school in Pakistan and has an advanced-level certificate with passes in three A-level examinations. Ali learned by reading university brochures carefully that University A will give him credit for each advanced-level examination he has completed with high marks. With this credit, he will be admitted at the sophomore level. It will take Ali less time to get his bachelor's degree. He will need to take fewer courses at the undergraduate level. After completing his bachelor's degree in the United States, Ali wants to continue for a master's degree.

Note: Each university makes its own decisions about awarding transfer credit for study at another university. If Ali decides to attend a different university, for example University B, he may find that he will need to enter as a freshman.

Practice

EXERCISE 1-1

Read this profile of an American student who has just graduated from high school.

My name is Michelle Brown, and I graduated from Huron High School this year. I was busy with classes, extracurricular activities, and part-time jobs outside school. My senior year I studied physics, psychology, math analysis, history, American literature, art and music of Europe, and physical education lifesaving. I was elected to student government, and I was a cheerleader for my school's football team. Outside of school, I worked as a salesperson in a department store.

Last fall I received stacks of college pamphlets in the mail after taking my SATs and ACTs. Although I hadn't visited any of the schools, I read the information carefully and finally narrowed down my choices to five small liberal arts colleges. I applied to them in January and was accepted at all five for the fall. I chose Denison University in southern Ohio. The campus is beautiful, the students were friendly during my visit, and my financial aid packet is large. Denison is a small school, with just twenty-two hundred students. Classes will be small, professors accessible, and extracurricular activities plentiful.

Check your understanding of this special vocabulary:

cheerleader: a person who directs organized cheering for a sports team

extracurricular activities: activities that take place after school and do not receive academic credit

financial aid packet: an award of money (which may include grants, loans, and a campus job) from a university to help a student pay for his or her education)

liberal arts: a general university program

lifesaving: a swimming class that teaches how to save people from drowning

SATs and ACTs: standardized tests of verbal and math skills

semester: a term of study, usually fifteen or sixteen weeks

stacks of college pamphlets: a lot of information about colleges

student government: an organization of student representatives that manages student activities on campus

Now compare Michelle's experience with your own. In what ways are they the same? In what ways are they different?

Same   **Different**

APPLYING FOR GRADUATE STUDY IN THE UNITED STATES

If you are considering going to the United States to study after you obtain a university degree, you will apply for graduate study. The general requirements for graduate study are similar for all universities. However, the forms, documents, and deadlines for applying vary from one university to another.

Practice

EXERCISE 1-2

Read the information about graduate admission requirements from this brochure from the University of Houston. Then use the information to fill in the blanks in the paragraph on the next page.

Graduate Admission Requirements for International Students

General Requirements

The University of Houston bases admission of international students to graduate study on the following general factors.

- Completion of a four-year bachelor's degree or its equivalent from an accredited college or university
- Scholastic performance showing high probability of success

- Evidence of satisfactory English proficiency
- Satisfactory scores on the appropriate standardized admission test
- Evidence of ability to maintain a full course of study while at the university. All students are required to enroll in a minimum of 12 semester credit hours each academic semester, except for natural sciences and mathematics majors who are required to enroll in a minimum of 15 semester credit hours.

More specific requirements for each college can be found on the following pages.

Graduate applications are processed through the combined efforts of the International Student Section of the Office of Admissions and the individual colleges and departments. The Office of Admissions is primarily responsible for the gathering and evaluation of documents which are then forwarded to the colleges and departments where they are reviewed and an admission decision is made. Because admission requirements are subject to change, applications are considered for specific semesters only. If you do not enroll for the original semester for which you applied, you must submit a letter requesting that your application be considered for a subsequent semester. You will also have to re-submit an application fee and any additional documents prior to an admission decision.

Grade Point Average

To qualify for admission to graduate school, you must have a four-year degree from a properly accredited college or university and above average grades in your previous studies. In US terms, you must have at least a B average (A = 4.0, B = 3.0, C = 2.0, D = 1.0, F = 0.0).

Transcripts

To apply, you must submit evidence of satisfactory completion of college- or university-level studies, including a complete set of school transcripts and diplomas. The transcripts should indicate the date studies were undertaken, the subjects covered and grades or marks earned in each subject. They must be official, sent directly to University of Houston from the granting institution and certified by that insitution. You must submit one copy in the original language as well as an official translation into English.

Standardized Test Requirement

The College of Architecture, the College of Education, the Cullen College of Engineering, the College of Humanities and Fine Arts, the College of Natural Sciences and Mathematics, the College of Optometry, the College of Pharmacy, and the College of Social Sciences require applicants to take the Graduate Record Examination (GRE). Many departments also require advanced (subject) tests. For specific admission requirements for your intended major, please contact the department of your major. All test scores should be sent directly to the International Student Section of the Office of Admissions. For information on the GRE, write:

Graduate Record Examination
Educational Testing Service
1947 Center Street
Berkeley, California 94704
USA

The College of Business Administration requires all applicants to take the Graduate Management Aptitude Test (GMAT). Ph.D. candidates may submit either the GMAT or the GRE. For information on the GMAT and the GRE, contact:

Educational Testing Service
P.O. Box 955
Princeton, New Jersey 08540
USA

Graduate admission to a U.S. university is based on several _____ .

Each student must have completed a _____ degree, have above average _____ in undergraduate studies, and have _____ English proficiency. Most applicants to graduate schools are expected to have taken the Graduate Record Examination (GRE), which is a _____ academic skills test. University students are expected to take at least twelve credits each semester in order to be _____-time students.

Questions and Answers

I have a bachelor's degree. Can I get another one from a U.S. university?

Most universities do not admit students for a second bachelor's degree. A student who has a bachelor's degree and wants to study a new subject area should apply for graduate study in the new area. The student may be admitted conditionally to graduate study in the new area, but may have to take some undergraduate-level courses to make up for any gaps in knowledge in the new subject area. The undergraduate courses will not be counted as credit for the master's degree.

I have a master's degree in mathematics from a university in my native country. I want to get my Ph.D. in mathematics in the United States. I don't need English to study math. Why do I need to do well on an English test in order to be admitted?

There are many reasons why you must be proficient in English:

- Your professors will need to discuss your work with you.
- You will need to communicate with your fellow students.
- You may want to submit articles to journals that are published in English.
- You may want to present your research at international conferences.
- You may want or need financial support from the university. Since most financial assistance for graduate students is through teaching fellowship awards, you will need English to communicate with the undergraduate American students in your assigned class.

UNDERSTANDING THE APPLICATION PROCESS

Whether you are applying for undergraduate or graduate study, the process is similar. You have to

- Become informed about U.S. universities and courses
- Write to several universities for information
- Read all the information sent by the universities
- Choose and apply to some universities
- Accept your best offer
- Go to the United States to study!

The application process takes *time*. Most advisers suggest that you make a time schedule. If you want to go to an American university in September, you should start your research at least a year before that.

The application process also takes *money*. You may have to write to several universities, which will require a lot of postage. You will have to make photocopies of many forms and also pay for translations and notarization (having a public official certify that your signature or document is genuine). In addition, most universities charge an application fee of about $10 to $65.

Finally, the application process takes *patience*. Even if you send your letters and applications by air mail, there can always be unexpected problems—such as a postal workers' strike!

International students who are now in the United States say that the most difficult parts of the application process were

- Getting an overall picture of what they had to do
- Describing the educational systems of their native country
- Writing a "statement of purpose" essay
- Understanding complicated instructions
- Getting steps completed by the deadlines
- Determining if they had the right qualifications
- Arranging to take the necessary tests (e.g., TOEFL, GRE, SAT)
- Explaining special circumstances or problems

As you work through this book, you will learn how to avoid problems with these and other parts of the application process. You will also find tips on how to get everything done on time and how to build a complete, successful application file.

Remember, the most important thing you can do is to plan ahead!

Getting the Whole Picture

Many international students say they had trouble getting a complete picture of the application process. Unfortunately, they understood the whole process only when they had *finished* it, and they wished they had understood it from the *beginning!*

The flowchart in Figure 1B gives you a complete picture of the application process from beginning to end. The process is similar for every university, although each university has its own requirements. For example, University A requires a 550 TOEFL score, whereas University B requires a 600; University A has an application deadline of January 15, but University B's deadline is February 15. You must read the instructions on each university's forms very carefully to see if you have sufficient qualifications, finances, and time to apply.

Figure 1B.   The Application Process

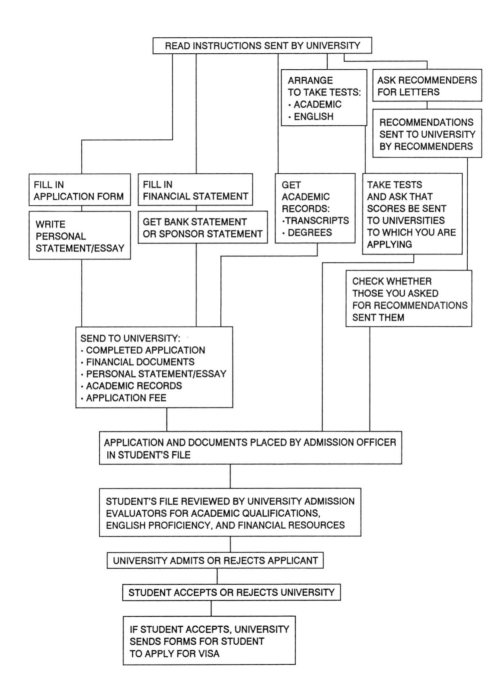

Practice

EXERCISE 1-3

Look at each step in Figure 1B, the flowchart of the application process. Which steps will be easy for you to complete? Put check marks next to the easy steps and stars next to the difficult steps.

EXERCISE 1-4

Formal language is often used in application forms. Match each formal direction to the explanation that tells what it means.

1. Submit official test results.

2. Send letters of recommendation.

3. Enclose official transcripts of last four years of study.

4. Submit a certified bank letter or credit reference.

5. Attach a certified check or money order in U.S. dollars, payable to the university.

6. Provide a notarized translation.

a. Ask your current or previous school to write a statement on official paper giving the dates that you attended classes, the names of courses you took, and the grades/marks you received. This document must be signed by an official of the institution, usually with an official seal.

b. You may need to go to the bank to obtain a money order, or ask a friend already in the United States to write a check for you. The check or money order must be in U.S. dollars and it must give the name of the university as the one who may cash the check.

c. Find out which tests (e.g., TOEFL, SAT, GRE) you need to take, and when and where the tests are given. On the test application forms, write the name of each university that you are applying to. Before taking a test, you will have the opportunity to check and change this information if necessary.

d. Go to your bank and ask for a letter or form showing that you have enough money to support yourself during the time you will be in the United States.

e. If your documents (such as school records, diplomas, bank statements, and letters of recommendation) are not in English, you must have them translated officially.

f. Ask teachers or counselors to write letters recommending you for university study. Ask as many recommenders as you need and then check later that each one has written and mailed a letter.

EXERCISE 1-5

Make an application time schedule showing what you will need to do and when each step must be done. Add as many rows as you need.

Tasks   **Months**

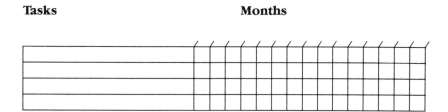

Questions and Answers

Why do the words *official, certified,* and *notarized* appear so many times in the application instructions?

Admissions officers must check for fraud. They must make sure you have the qualifications, test scores, and money you say you have. Admissions officers won't accept copies of documents because it is easy to change scores, dates, and other information when you make a photocopy. You will need to find out the system your country uses for proving that documents are genuine.

CHAPTER TWO

How Do I Get Application and Program Information?

- ► CHOOSING UNIVERSITIES TO WRITE TO

- ► WRITING TO UNIVERSITY ADMISSIONS OFFICES

- ► GETTING INFORMATION ABOUT GRADUATE PROGRAMS

- ► EVALUATING GRADUATE PROGRAMS

CHOOSING UNIVERSITIES TO WRITE TO

Before you write to any universities, you first need information. But there are over 3,000 institutions of higher education, and for many students this choice is overwhelming. They don't know where to begin.

Some students begin by

- Talking or writing to a friend who has studied in the United States
- Meeting with an educational counselor
- Writing to or visiting a binational center
- Going to an educational library that has reference books, university bulletins, and video and computer programs
- Checking to see if there is a university alumni association in the area and talking to graduates of the university

These are some of the things students think about when they choose the colleges they will apply to.

Do I have all the necessary qualifications?

Do I have enough money?

Do I know anyone who has been there and who has enjoyed it?

Do I like the location, the size, and the reputation of the university?

Do I have sufficient English language skills?

Does the college or university have an English as a second language program?

The United States Information Service (USIS) can help you research which schools to write to. USIS offers public training sessions, counseling, interviews, and predeparture orientation. You can write to

Library Programs Division
USIA
Washington, D.C. 20547
USA

for a list of the locations of USIS offices worldwide.

In the USIS offices are reference books, videos, and information on local scholarships and awards. Reference books include handbooks, directories, guide books, and advice books. These resources and counselors can help you make a choice.

By reading reference books, you will get an idea of the different types of schools, colleges, and universities of higher education in the United States. In this book we usually use the word *university* to mean any kind of education after secondary (high school). You will see in the reference books, however, that—

- Trade education and other short training programs are usually called schools or institutes
- Most two-year schools are called community colleges or junior colleges: e.g., Seattle Community College
- Four-year schools are called colleges or universities: e.g., Bucknell University
- Schools with four-year undergraduate programs and graduate programs are usually called universities: e.g., the University of California
- Schools within a larger university are called schools, colleges, or faculties: e.g., School of Education, College of Education, Faculty of Education
- Graduate professional programs are usually called schools: e.g., Medical School, Law School

Reference books, such as those published by Peterson's Guides and by Barron's Educational Series, provide comprehensive information on the many U.S. universities. Profiles of universities usually include information on the following:

- How it is funded—with private or public funds
- Size of student population and number of instructors
- Where it is located
- Number of books in the university's libraries
- What major areas of study are offered
- What degrees are awarded
- Expenses—fees and living costs

Reference books often categorize universities according to how difficult it is for an American student to be admitted to undergraduate study. The most competitive universities are those most difficult to enter. These universities usually offer admission to only those students with excellent academic backgrounds. The ranking of schools from most competitive to least competitive is also based on the ratio of number of U.S. students applying to be freshmen to number accepted.

Many universities, including those with moderate or less competitive admission rankings, provide quality programs of education. State universities are supported with public tax revenues and admit the most students.

International students are admitted to all kinds of universities. The majority of international students attend large universities, but many smaller universities encourage applications from international students. (Appendix 3 lists U.S. universities with the most international students.)

Practice

EXERCISE 2-1

Read the directory profile on Indiana University. This profile is from a reference book that lists many universities for students who want to know about undergraduate programs in the United States. Find the specific facts given in this directory listing. The first two are done as examples.

INDIANA UNIVERSITY BLOOMINGTON, Bloomington
General Information State-supported coed university. Awards A, B, M, D. City setting. Entrance for U.S. students: moderately difficult. *Enrollment* 33,776 total; 25,386 undergraduates from 114 countries, 53% women, 2% international students. *Faculty* 1,595; 87% of full-time faculty have doctoral degrees. *Library Holdings* 4.8 million bound volumes, 2 million titles on microform. *Computer Facilities* Computer terminals/PCs available for student use: 407, located in computer center, student center, library, dormitories, academic buildings. *Majors* Total: 138.

Information for International Students For fall 1988: 493 international students applied, 425 enrolled. Students can start in January, May, June, or August. *Admissions Tests* Required: SAT, TOEFL. Recommended: Achievement Tests, *Application Deadline* 2/15. Transfers accepted from institutions abroad. *Costs and Aid* Tuition and fees (1989-90), $6086; room and board, $2945 (on campus). Need-based, non-need grants available. For fall 1988, 9 applied for grants, 6 were awarded grants, ($500 average). *Housing On-campus* housing guaranteed, also available during summer. *Services* International student advisor on campus. Full-time ESL program on campus; part-time program also available. *Contact* Associate Dean and Director of International Student Services, Indiana University Bloomington, 306 Franklin Hall, Bloomington, IN 47405 USA. Telephone: 812-855-9086. Cable: INDVERS. Telex: 27-2279.

From: *Applying to Colleges and Universities in the United States, Fourth Edition.* Copyright 1989 Peterson's Guides.

1. Location of university — Bloomington, Indiana

2. ZIP code for mail — IN 47405

3. Private or state university? _____

4. Types of degrees awarded _____

5. Number of full-time faculty _____

6. Size of library collection _____

7. Total number of students _____

8. Number of undergraduate students _____

9. Number of countries represented in student enrollment _____

10. Entrance difficulty for U.S. students _____

11. Tests required of international students _____

12. Application deadline   _____

13. Number of areas of study avail-
    able   _____

14. Tuition and fees for study   _____

15. Room and board cost   _____

16. Phone number of International
    Students' Office   _____

17. Name/title of person to contact
    for application   _____

18. Address where to write for appli-
    cation   _____

WRITING TO UNIVERSITY ADMISSIONS OFFICES

There are two ways to get information from colleges and universities. You can

1. Use a preliminary application form
2. Write a letter

Each university has its own admissions system. You need to send a form or letter to each university. You can get names and addresses of universities from the reference books.

If you don't have a reference book with addresses, you can write to

International Admissions Officer
Undergraduate (or Graduate) Studies
XXXXX University
City, State ZIP
USA

If you are interested in a professional program, write that on the envelope, too. For example:

International Admissions Officer
Graduate Dental Programs
XXXXX University
City, State ZIP
USA

If you want information about graduate programs in a specific area, you can write directly to the department. For example—

Graduate Admissions
Chemistry Department
XXXXX University
City, State ZIP
USA

If you want to study the English language only, write

English Language Study Program
XXXXX University
City, State ZIP
USA

Make sure your return address is on the envelope and on your form or letter. Use a typewriter or print. Your writing must be easy to read or your envelope will not be delivered to the proper destination.

In all your correspondence with a university, you should be consistent (use the same style) and make sure that it is clear which is your family name. (Look in Appendix 1 for more about names.)

Using a Preliminary Application Form

A preliminary application form is *not* an application for admission. It is a form used for getting information from a university. It is sometimes called a Request for Application Material form.

You can get preliminary application forms from a USIS office or an international education information office. The purpose of the form is to provide information to the university to help the university decide whether to send you application information.

A copy of the form is sent to each university. You do not send any money with the form. You do not send any academic or financial documents.

A student applying for graduate study should provide detailed information about academic background, list work experience related to the intended field of study, and identify the intended field of study. It helps a university to know whether they have the special type of program you want.

On preliminary application forms you must give dates about yourself: your birthdate, dates of your previous education, and dates related to when you want to begin university study in the United States.

The standard U.S. style for dates is:

Birthdate (month/day/year)	7/15/72
Enrollment date (month/year) or (term/year)	September 1992
	Fall 1992
Graduation date (month/year)	April 1992
Date attended (year–year)	1985–88

It is not necessary to use a preliminary application form. The form is an easy, convenient way to get information, but it is fine to write a letter including the same information.

Writing a Request for Information Letter

A request for information letter is another way to get the information and application forms from a U.S. university. Your letter should be

Clearly organized

Neatly written

In good English

It should include

What you want to study

When you want to begin your study in the United States

Brief information about your educational background

Information about standard tests you have taken

How you plan to pay for your education

Your name and address

Some college information reference books include the name and address of the person you should write for an application. You address your letter and envelope to that person.

One coordinator of international admissions advised

Urge prospective students to provide *details* of academic achievement with the initial inquiry. We require this information for "preliminary review."

Also urge inquiries *before* (or at the latest) in September of the year before the student wants to enroll.

Practice

EXERCISE 2-2

Read through Figure 2A, the request for application materials that was completed by a Japanese student. There are sixteen sections on the form. Find the section(s) that gives the following information about the student.

1. His name
2. His address
3. When he was born
4. His marital status
5. What his native language is
6. How he will pay for his studies
7. His background in English
8. What degree he wants to study and when he can begin
9. His educational background
10. What tests he has taken or plans to take

Figure 2A.   A Completed Request for Application Materials

To the applicant: To obtain application forms for admission to a U.S. school, college, or university, complete this form and send it AIR MAIL to the Admissions Officer at the institution that interests you. It is best to apply at least one academic year before you expect to begin your U.S. studies.

IMPORTANT
- Read the ENTIRE form before answering the questions.
- PRINT your answers in ink, or use a typewriter
- Answer in English, except for names of degrees, titles, certificates, etc.
   Give the names of these in the original language(s), using the roman alphabet
- Do NOT attach documents at this stage.

REQUEST FOR APPLICATION MATERIAL

Dear Admissions Officer:

I would like to apply for admission to your institution. My qualifications are outlined below. If they meet your requirements, please send me an application form and information about foreign student admissions. Thank you.

1. My name: ___Ichiro_____(Tanaka)_____
   First name   Middle name   Last name(s)
   Important: Please circle family name

2. My address for reply: _5-318 Katori-cho_____
   Nagoya, Japan 453

3. Date of Birth ___7/15/73_____   4. ☒ Male   ☐ Female   5. ☐ Married   ☒ Unmarried
   (Month/Day/Year)

6. Citizen of___Japan_____   7. Primary language spoken in my home: _Japanese_____.
   Country

8. I wish to enroll in a (check one.) ☐ associate degree   ☒ bachelor's degree   ☐ master's degree

   ☐ doctoral degree program in _____ for the term beginning ☒ Fall   ☐ Spring, 19__93__
   (field of study)

9. I have completed ___7___ years of formal study of the English language at (list institutions and dates): _____
   Nagoya Junior High (86-89); Nagoya Senior High (89-90), (91-present),
   ELS International (Summer,1990) ; Northside High, Fort Wayne, Indiana (90-91)

   TOEFL score, if available __590_____

10. I expect to have an estimated $ __16,000_____ in U.S. dollars available each year for tuition and expenses in the United States. The source of this income is: _____
    my family

11. *Please check one:*   ☐ I plan to   ☐ I do NOT plan to   request financial aid from your institution.

    If financial aid is not available, I ☐ do   ☐ do not wish to be considered for admission.

12. I have taken, or plan to take, the following standardized tests. (Give dates taken or when you expect to take them)

    ☒ TOEFL _4/91___   ☐ ACT _____   ☐ Michigan Language Test_____
         Date   Date   Date

    ☐ GRE _____   ☒ SAT _5/92___   ☐ Achievement tests _____
         Date   Date   Field of Study/Date

    ☐ GMAT _____   ☐ TSE* _____   _____
         Date   Date   Field of Study/Date

    Other standardized tests, e.g., O levels, I have taken or plan to take:
         Name of test   *Date*

    _____

    _____

    _____

*The Test of Spoken English is especially important for graduate students seeking teaching assistantships

(Please turn over)

Figure 2A.—Continued

13. **EDUCATION**
(Please provide information for all institutions attended since primary school, beginning with the most recent. Attach additional page if necessary.)

Name of School, College or University	City, Country	Dates Attended 19___ to 19___	Major Field of Study	Primary Language of Instruction	Degree, Diploma, Title Earned or Expected *(Do not translate into English)*	Date Earned or Expected
Nagoya Senior High School	Nagoya, Japan	1989–1990 1991–present		Japanese	Graduation certificate	April 1992
Northside High School	Fort Wayne, Indiana USA	1990–1991		English		
Nagoya Junior High School	Nagoya, Japan	1986–1989		Japanese	Graduation certificate	April 1989

14. Grade average _____ or class rank ___25___ in a class of ___400___ at institution currently or most recently attended.

15. I propose to undertake the following plan of study in the United States: *(This information is required for graduate students, optional but desirable for undergraduate applicants).*

During 1989-90 I was an exchange student at an American high school. I really enjoyed studying American history at that time and would like to study U.S. history and economics at a U.S. university. While I was in the U.S. I had the chance to improve my English in class and outside of class. I was a member of school orchestra and the tennis team. I have played violin since I was six years old. At Nagoya High School I am the leader of the Sports Club and have played in several national tennis matches.

16. I would like to receive information on your English as a Second Language programs at your school.   ☐ Yes   ☒ No

Tanaka Ichiro
Signature

January 15, 1992
Date

NOTE: This form is distributed by the Institute of International Education to assist U.S. colleges and universities and foreign students applying for admission to them. Its use does not imply sponsorship by IIE.

EXERCISE 2-3

Read this college profile and the request for information letter in Figure 2B. Then answer the questions that follow.

UNIVERSITY OF TEXAS AT AUSTIN, Austin
General Information State-supported coed university. Awards B, M, D. City setting. Entrance for U.S. students: moderately difficult. *Enrollment* 50,107 total; 38,145 undergraduates from 91 countries, 48% women, 3% international students. *Faculty* 2,301; 80% of full-time faculty have doctoral degrees. *Library Holdings* 5.8 million bound volumes, 4.0 million titles on microform. *Computer Facilities* Computer terminals/PCs available for student use: 12,000, located in computer center, student center, library, dormitories. *Majors* Total: 126.

Information for International Students For fall 1988: 4,322 international students applied, 1410 were accepted, 1000 enrolled. Students can start in January, June, or August. *Admissions Tests* Required: SAT, TOEFL (minimum score: 550). *Application Deadline* 4/1. Transfers accepted from institutions abroad. *Costs and Aid* Tuition and fees (1988-89), $3600; room and board, $3300 (on campus). Non-need grants available ($200 average). *Housing* Available during summer. *Services* International student advisor on campus. Full-time ESL program on campus. *Contact* Associate Director of Admissions, University of Texas at Austin, Main 7, Austin, TX 78712 USA. Telephone: 512-471-1711.

From: *Applying to Colleges and Universities in the United States, Fourth Edition.* Copyright 1989 Peterson's Guides.

Figure 2B.   A Request for Information Letter

P.O. Box 5438
Jeddah, Saudi Arabia
February 3, 1992

Associate Director of Admissions
University of Texas at Austin
Austin, TX 78712 USA

Dear Associate Director,

I am currently in my junior year at the International School here in Saudi Arabia. I am a citizen of Jordan. I have taken a college preparatory program. I am taking mathematics, physics and chemistry at the Higher Level for the International Baccalaureate. I have done particularly well in chemistry and physics classes and received the school Science Award last year. I expect to graduate in May 1993. I plan to begin my university study in Fall 1993, and I hope to study for a bachelor's degree in physics or engineering.

My native language is Arabic, but the language of instruction in my school is English. I plan to take the TOEFL and SAT in September.

My family has sufficient funds to support four years of study in the United States.

Please send me an application form and information about your college. Also, I may have an opportunity to visit the United States next summer. Could you please send me information about college visits?

Yours sincerely,

Ahmed Jamal
Ahmed Jamal

1. How will Ahmed Jamal pay for his tuition?
2. What exams will he take and when?
3. Why is he writing the letter?
4. What does he want to study and when?
5. What is his educational background?

EXERCISE 2-4

Write a letter requesting application information. It can be short, but it should include all the necessary information. You can use the same basic letter for each university to which you write for application information.

GETTING INFORMATION ABOUT GRADUATE PROGRAMS

The application process for graduate students is a little different from the process for undergraduates. Undergraduate applications are handled by one central office, and the admissions committee decides whether the student is qualified and whether they will make an offer.

Graduate applications are handled by a central office *and* the department. The central office reviews the student's basic qualifications, and the committee in the department decides whether to offer a place.

You may need a special application form. Different fields of study may have their own forms. For example, there may be separate forms for the College of Architecture, the School of Dentistry, etc.

You may also be eligible for financial aid. For example, if you already have a master's and wish to enroll as a Ph.D. student, you may be eligible for financial aid in your first year. In general, there is more financial aid available for Ph.D. students.

When you are considering applying to graduate school, write a postcard to the Graduate Admissions Advisor requesting information. Most programs will have a "packet" of materials that may give information such as

Addresses and phone numbers	Course descriptions
Size and resources of the department	Sources for scholarships
List of faculty and their specialties	Details of fellowships
Recent faculty publications	Requirements
Faculty teaching and research interests	Deadlines

Read the packet carefully and supplement it with discussions with professors who know the programs and with your own reading of journals to check on who is doing what research. You are looking for a "match" between (1) your qualifications and the university requirements, and (2) your interests and the focus of the department.

At the graduate level it is important to find the information that is right for you. You will be working in a specialized area, and some universities will have courses and instructors more suited to your professional interests. In your letter requesting an application form, you should give your qualifications, be very specific about your plans for graduate work, and state whether you are interested in a master's or doctorate.

When graduate students think about which university they want to go to, they will look at the work done by a particular department or professor. They may get this information from reading the literature in their field, or by talking to their teachers or other students who have studied there.

You may have read books or journal articles by a certain professor and decide you would like to study with that person. You may want to write to that professor because

- Professors in America frequently move from one university to another. It's a good idea to check that the professor who interests you will be at the university at the time you want to study there.
- If you have work or research experience, or have published in an area similar to that of a particular professor, you may wish to establish contact with that professor.
- When your application is discussed by a departmental committee consisting of faculty, it can be helpful if a professor knows more about you.

Professors receive a number of letters from prospective students. Some professors write a personal reply; some give the letters to an admissions secretary who sends the application forms. Figures 2C and 2D show an exchange between one student and a professor of oceanography.

Practice

EXERCISE 2-5

When In Sun Kim wanted to do graduate study in the United States, he wrote to several U.S. professors working in his subject area, oceanography. Tell which paragraph or paragraphs in his letter (Figure 2C) explain each of the following:

1. His first degree
2. His second degree
3. His current work
4. His general qualifications
5. His English proficiency
6. His recent research
7. His teacher's name
8. His financial situation

Figure 2C.   A Student's Letter to a Professor

Institute of Oceanology
P.O. Box 8970
Pusan, Korea
July 12, 1992

Dr. J. Smith
College of Oceanography
Northern State University
Northville, OR 12345
USA

Dear Dr. Smith,

My name is In Sun Kim. I was born on January 5, 1964, in Pusan, Korea. In 1986, I graduated from South University, where I majored in fluid mechanics. I was admitted to the Mechanical Engineering Department of Central University and majored in Computational Fluid Mechanics. Two and a half years late, I got an M.Sc. degree and was admitted to the Department of Physical Oceanography of the Institute of Oceanology to complete my Ph.D. program under the guidance of Prof. Jong Sung.

I have completed all the required courses with satisfied scores in both my undergraduate and my graduate courses. I took the TOEFL on March 5, 1991, with a score of 550. With my English training, I should have no difficulty either in functioning on a daily bodies or in participating fully in graduate studies. Up to now, all things were going very well with me. I've read some books on physical oceanography and done some works on it. Moreover, I took part in a cruise to the estuary of the Main River and a part of the area of the East China Sea. On that cruise, I took current meter observations and I hope to publish an article on this.

I've read and admired your papers in the literature for a long time. I would very much appreciate an opportunity to study under your guidance as soon as possible and I'm sure I would make progress in my future career. It's Prof. Sung's wish and my great desire that I can complete my education in US. Since my university is short of foreign exchange, it is impossible for me to get a scholarship from here. I hope I can get a financial support at your department, especially for the first year. I hope to hear good news from you soon.

Very sincerely yours,

In Sun Kim
In Sun Kim

EXERCISE 2-6

Read the letter (Figure 2D) from the professor. Answer the questions here and on page 27 about what information is included.

Paragraph 1

1. Will In Sun Kim receive an information package?

2. Does the university term begin in September?

3. Can In Sun Kim go to the university in September?

4. Can he get a scholarship?

Figure 2D.   The Professor's Reply to the Student's Letter

College of Oceanography,
Northern State University,
Northville, OR 12345
August 18, 1992

Mr. In Sun Kim
Institute of Oceanology
P.O. Box 8970
Pusan, Korea

Dear Mr. Kim,

(1) Thank you for your letter expressing an interest in studying with me. I have arranged for our standard information packet and admissions material to be mailed to you in a separate envelope. Unfortunately, our fall academic term begins in about a month. It is impossible to admit you on such short notice. In addition, our scholarships and research assistantships are already fully committed for the fall term.

(2) It is possible to admit you in January, but we do not encourage our students to begin in the middle of an academic year unless they are unusually well-prepared and have a strong need to begin their studies as soon as possible. Since you already have a master's degree, you could probably be successful in your studies if you began in January, but it would be hard. You can indicate on your admissions form what you wish to do.

(3) At present, I have more students than I have money to support them, but fortunately, one student has been awarded a teaching assistantship by the department. Another student will be graduating in a year, and this will free a research assistant position. I am very confident that we will be able to offer you financial support for the academic year beginning a year from this coming September, but finding support beginning in January will be hard unless your accomplishments are exceptional.

(4) I am pleased that you have taken the TOEFL test (an English proficiency test is required of all students whose first language is not English), but I noticed several mistakes in your letter (although I have no trouble understanding your meaning). We have many students whose native language is not English and they generally have been good students here, but many have trouble with spoken English. I would encourage you to study English very hard between now and when you come to America.

(5) Numerical computation is an important part of our work here and I would encourage you to gain practice in FORTRAN programming and in the application of numerical algorithms. The department has three VAX minicomputers and the College is about to purchase an Alliant mainframe computer. The university has an excellent computer system with several machines connected by a campus wide network. The Alliant will be one host on the network: others include the supercomputers at the National Center for Atmospheric Research in Boulder and the CRAY XMP supercomputer at San Diego, which are accessed through high-speed satellite links. The names of the American computers may not mean much to you, but the point is that we have very good computer facilities and our students make heavy use of them.

(6) Admission to our graduate program is competitive. Since I have not seen your transcripts or letters of recommendation, I cannot say whether we will admit you or not. However, your letter indicates that you have an excellent background in fluid mechanics and oceanography. I am pleased that you are interested in studying with me.

Figure 2D.—Continued

⑦ If you have any questions either about the admission process or about scientific matters or your studies here, please write me.

With best wishes,

Jeramy Smith

Jeramy Smith

Paragraph 2

5. Can In Sun Kim start his studies in January?
6. Does the professor advise him to come in January?
7. How hard will the work be if he starts in January?
8. Where should In Sun Kim say what term he wants to start?

Paragraph 3

9. What job does In Sun Kim have the best chance to get?
10. Under what conditions may he get support in January?
11. Is the professor talking about getting money for students in the form of a grant, a scholarship, a loan, or a part-time job in the university?

Paragraph 4

12. Are all students required to take the TOEFL?
13. Have nonnative speakers of English succeeded in studying at the university?
14. With what form of English do many international students have trouble?

Paragraph 5

15. Does the university have good computer facilities?
16. What computer knowledge would prepare Kim for his studies?

Paragraphs 6 and 7

17. Is it difficult to get into the graduate program?
18. Is the professor offering Kim a place?
19. Can Kim write to this professor again with questions?

EVALUATING GRADUATE PROGRAMS

You will need to know which graduate programs are appropriate for you and will enable you to meet your goals.

Look at reference books, like *Peterson's Guides to Graduate Studies* for the top schools in your field. Look for the facilities that you need:

- Computer facilities
- Library size and specialization
- Reputation in your field
- Publication rate
- Curriculum

Read recent journals. Take notes on articles you are interested in and write the names of those who did good research and communicated information about it well.

- Look at where the authors are working or where they were trained.
- Check the dates of the journals—once more, remember that some professors move on and may not be at the same university anymore.
- Make sure that your interests are similar to those of the department to which you are applying.

It's important to find out what the present program is like. Sometimes you can't get reliable answers to vital questions from reading publications. If possible,

- Work with faculty in your country who have good contacts in the United States.
- Get in touch with faculty who have been to international conferences and find out their opinions about different departments.

The following show the kind of questions you should ask. First try to find the answers in the information packets you receive.

1. What kind of environment is it?
   (Fiercely competitive environment, socially isolated, open and supportive, student-friendly, etc.)
2. What kind of funding and support does it offer students?
   (For average students as well as the stars?)
3. How do students do when they leave the program?
   (Do they immediately find placement, or is it hard to get placed?)

If the above information is not given in the packet sent to you by the university, write to the department yourself:

- Address your inquiry to the Graduate Student Advisor of the department.
- Later you may wish to write to a particular professor to clarify what the requirements for admission are and also the kind of research they have planned. (Take another look at Figures 2C and 2D.)
- You could also ask for the name of a student you could write to.

With information from all these sources, you can build up a picture of the department you may be working in for a number of years. It is important to get a realistic view of the department. Is it growing? declining? in chaos?

Questions and Answers

Can I send the same preapplication form to each university?
Yes. It will save you a lot of time. Make photocopies if you can. But if you receive a preapplication form from a particular university, you should return the form only to that university.

What does the university do with my preapplication form?
They read it to see if you are generally qualified. If you are, they will send you an application for admission and an information brochure. If you are not, you may not hear from them.

How soon will I get a reply to my preapplication form?

If you have written your name and address clearly and you sent it air mail, you should receive the information within a month or less.

Where do I send my preapplication form or my letter requesting materials?

Review the information on pages 17–18. Be sure to state clearly on the envelope whether you want to enter an undergraduate or a graduate program.

Why can't I just write "Please send me an application form for your university"?

You are telling the university in a letter whether you have the basic qualifications. A university will usually not send an application form to everyone who asks, but uses a preapplication form to screen qualified applicants. It may save time to include as much relevant information as you can, as they will then not need to send you the preapplication form—you have told them the basic information about yourself in your letter.

Also, it will help you get the correct application form. Some universities have different application forms for foreign undergraduate applicants and foreign graduate applicants. Also, there are special application forms for certain colleges such as the College of Architecture or College of Music within a larger university system.

Do I need the street address of the admissions office?

No, it's not necessary, but you should send your letter to the *correct* admissions office. It is important that it is clear in your letter whether you want to enter an undergraduate or a graduate program.

Do I need to type my letters?

No, but write or print clearly. Admissions officers cannot send you information unless they can read your letter.

I'm not sure what to write, and my English is poor. Will the professor be offended, and think I'm a weak student?

Professors understand that English is not your first language. In fact, many prefer to see a letter written by you and not one written by your English teacher. It gives them a better idea of your level of English. Just make sure you put in all the necessary information—see Chapter 1.

If the professor doesn't answer my letter, what does it mean?

Did you receive the application form? If so, then the professor sent your letter to the right office, so go ahead and apply. Maybe the professor had no time to write a personal letter back to you.

Courtesy of North Carolina State University

CHAPTER THREE

What Tests Do I Need to Take?

- ► GENERAL TESTING INFORMATION

- ► ENGLISH LANGUAGE TESTS

- ► UNDERGRADUATE APPLICANTS—ACADEMIC TESTS

- ► GRADUATE APPLICANTS—ACADEMIC TESTS AND SPECIAL ENGLISH TESTS

GENERAL TESTING INFORMATION

Most American universities require that an applicant take certain tests *before* the application for admission can be considered. The tests that each university requires are listed in the information bulletin of the university. All applicants may need to take some kind of *academic* test. Additionally, most international students need to take an *English language proficiency* test.

Because of the general structure of education in the United States, the general quality of education differs in various schools. The knowledge and skills of students may depend on their educational experiences.

In many countries of the world, secondary school students must take national examinations (tests) for entrance into a university. The tests are given by a government agency or ministry of education. Students with the highest scores are allowed entrance into the university system. Standards vary from one country to another. Some have difficult university entrance examinations; others are easier.

In the United States there are no national university entrance examinations (tests). Each college or university decides which students they want to admit. In order to decide whether a student should be admitted, the admissions officers need to know about a student's educational background. How can they compare the backgrounds of students who have attended different schools? To help them compare students' qualifications for study, admissions officers have found that a common measure is helpful. The common measures are test scores.

In the United States the external tests students take for university admission are prepared and administered by testing organizations. The testing organizations are not government organizations. The largest testing organization is ETS (Educational Testing Service). Its main office is in Princeton, New Jersey. The ETS organization administers academic tests such as the SAT and GRE and English tests such as TOEFL and TSE.

A student must register with the testing organization to take a required test. The student pays a fee to the testing organization for this service. After the student takes the test, the organization scores the test and sends the test results to the university. International students can take the tests in their home countries.

STUDENTS MUST PLAN AHEAD AND TAKE TESTS EARLY. A STUDENT'S SCORES MAY NOT BE HIGH ENOUGH THE FIRST TIME. STUDENTS SHOULD TAKE TESTS EARLY SO THAT THEY HAVE TIME TO TAKE THEM AGAIN IF NECESSARY. Students should be making plans to take tests long before they need the scores. When everything goes smoothly, it may take at least six months from the time a student writes for information until the scores arrive at the university.

Scores must arrive at the university admissions office **at about the same time** that the application for admission form arrives at the university office. If a university has a deadline of January 15 for the application for admission, then the student must have taken the tests at least two months before. After the test is taken, the examiner sends it to the testing organization for scoring. The testing organization sends the test results directly to the university.

Figure 3A. Tests for Admission Consideration

Name of Test and Test Maker	Content and Scoring	When Given Outside US
Undergraduate—Academic		
SAT (Scholastic Aptitude Test) College Board ATP Educational Testing Service Princeton, New Jersey	2 verbal sections 2 math sections 1 TSWE (Test of Written English) 1 experimental section (either verbal, math, or TSWE) The verbal and math section scores range from 200 to 800 each. Total score—low 400, high 1600. TSWE scored separately, 20–60	6 times a year, but in some countries less frequently. Usually November, December, January, March, May, June.
ACT (American College Testing Program) American College Testing Program Iowa City, Iowa	English Usage Test Mathematics Usage Test Social Studies Reading Natural Science Reading Each of the 4 parts scored from low 1 to high 36. The 4 parts are averaged to make a composite score.	4 times a year, but in some countries less frequently. Usually October, December, February, April.
Graduate—Academic		
GRE General Test (Graduate Record Examinations) ETS—Education Testing Service Princeton, New Jersey	6 sections: 2 verbal sections 2 math sections 2 analytical sections 1 experimental section (not included in score) Each of 3 types of sections scored 200 low–800 high.	5 times a year, but in some countries less frequently. Usually October, December, February, April, June.
GRE Subject Tests	There are 17 different subject tests. Each subject test is intended for students who majored in that subject as an undergraduate.	4 times a year (never in June). Given on afternoon of dates when GRE General given in morning.
ENGLISH LANGUAGE PROFICIENCY TESTS (same for undergraduate and graduate applicants)		
TOEFL (Test of English as a Foreign Language) Educational Testing Service Princeton, New Jersey	Listening Comprehension Structure and Written Expression Vocabulary and Reading Scores on each of 3 sections range from low 20 to high 68. Total average 200–677	12 times a year, less often in some countries.
TWE (Test of Written English)	Writing a short essay. Scored separately from TOEFL, Low 1–high 6.	4 times a year included with TOEFL
TSE-A (Test of Spoken English)	Seven sections Verbal answers to a variety of questions—answers are recorded on tape. Scored 0–3 on pronunciation grammar fluency Scored 0–300 on comprehensibility	Not part of TOEFL/TWE but given on some of the same test dates in some countries.
MELAB (Michigan English Language Assessment Battery) English Language Institute The University of Michigan Ann Arbor, Michigan	Written composition Listening comprehension Objective (grammar, cloze, reading, vocabulary) Scores on writing low 53 high 97 on listening 30 100 on objective 15 100 Final MELAB average 33 99 Optional oral interview, scored separately low 1– high 4 +.	Arranged as needed when student needs test.

Test scores sent directly to the university from the testing organization are **official test scores.** Scores sent to the student are student copies. The scores are the same, but universities want official test scores. A dishonest student might change his or her test scores before giving them to the university. Such behavior is wrong. Sometimes students try to get higher scores on tests by getting answers from another student. Such behavior is called cheating. Dishonest test behavior and untrue test scores can result in a student being asked to leave a university. If an admissions officer learns after admitting a student that the student's scores were false, the university may expel ("kick out") the student from the university.

Different universities ask for different tests, but most ask foreign students to take an English language test such as the TOEFL or MELAB. All graduates usually have to take the GRE. On the forms they ask you to give the

- Date
- Place
- Scores

Since there are sometimes delays in getting the official test scores, a university may accept a copy of your most recent test scores on a provisional basis even if you plan to take the test again. The university can begin processing your application with the provisional scores, but it will not make a final decision without the latest official scores.

You can find out which tests are required by reading the application instructions. Often they tell you

- The minimum score you need
- The time period your score is valid—for example, the test must have been taken within the last two years

When you need to take a test, you must get the test registration information. You may need to write a short letter to the test organization.

Date

Name of test organization

Address of test organization

City, State (or Country)

I wish to take (name of test) in (country). Please send me test registration information. My mailing address is:

Your name

Street or post office box

City, Country

Thank you.

Practice

Students often do not make it clear whether the tests have been taken—or at least arranged.–*Admissions Officer*

EXERCISE 3-1

This is a list of verbs from various application forms. They are used in the question that asks about your examination results. Which refer to the past? Which refer to the future? Write *Past* or *Future* after each verb.

1. will take   _____   4. have taken   _____
2. was taken   _____   5. have already taken   _____
3. will be taken   _____   6. plan to take   _____

EXERCISE 3-2

Read these sections from three application forms. Pretend that today is May 15, 1992. Complete the sentences on the next page with the correct form of the verb *to take.*

JUNKO KINOSHITA

If appropriate to the program to which you are applying, please indicate which examinations you have taken or plan to take in the future:

☐ GRE   Date_____ V_____ M_____ A_____

☐ GMAT   Date_____ V_____ M_____ T_____

☐ MAT   Date_____ T_____

☑ TOEFL* Date *March 1991* T *550*

      *See international graduate brochure for TOEFL requirement.

PARDIS NIKOOKAR

Objective test(s) you plan to take or have already taken:

Date of Test:

MTELP _____

TOEFL *June '92* _____

GMAT _____

GRE *July '92* _____

SANJAY KUMAR

EXAMINATIONS TAKEN OR SCHEDULED:	
Graduate Record Examination:	
☐ General Test	Date Taken/Will Take _____
☐ Subject Test in _____	Date Taken/Will Take _____
☒ Graduate Management Admission Test	~~Date Taken~~/Will Take *June 1992*
☒ Test of English as a Foreign Language *Score 560*	Date Taken/~~Will Take~~ *January 1992*
☐ Other *(specify test)* _____	Date Taken/Will Take _____

1. Junko _____ the TOEFL.

2. Pardis _____ the GRE and the TOEFL.

3. Sanjay _____ the TOEFL and _____ the GMAT.

EXERCISE 3-3

What stage are *you* at? Complete these sentences, inserting the correct form of *to take* and your own dates.

1. By _____ I _____ the TOEFL.

2. I _____ the TOEFL on _____.

3. I _____ the TOEFL.

Now complete this form for yourself.

Intended Ohio State Program and Program-related Information					
Intended Program (Graduate) or College (Undergraduate) — See list	Program Code (Graduate only)	Intended Area of Specialization	Indicate first Degree you wish to earn at OSU ☐ Bachelor's ☐ Master's ☐ Doctorate ☐ Master's/Doctorate	For office use only	Date Recd
Quarter you expect to enroll ☐ Summer (June) ☐ Winter (Jan) ☐ Autumn (Sept) ☐ Spring (Mar)	Calendar Year 199____	Campus Columbus	Check one of the categories below: 1 ☐ University Residence Hall Application Requested 2 ☐ Student Family Housing Application Requested 3 ☐ No University Housing Requested	Pgm. Yes No FTR ☐ ☐	App Fee Y ☐ N ☐ W ☐ Res R ☐ N ☐ F ☐
GRE if any	Date of Test Mo Yr	Verbal Score %	Quantitative Score %	Analytical Score %	Advanced Subject Name Score % Subscores 1. _____ 2. _____ 3. _____
GMAT if any	Date of Test Mo. Yr.	Verbal Score %	Quantitative Score %	Total Score %	For undergraduate applicants only: If The Ohio State University cannot offer you a favorable admissions decision, would you like to be contacted by other Ohio institutions which are interested in students with your background (if you check "yes," your name and application information will be made available to other interested institutions of higher education in Ohio) _____ NO _____ YES
TOEFL if any	Date of Test Mo. Yr.	Section 1	Section 2 Section 3 Total Writing		

EXERCISE 3-4

How does any student know which test must be taken? BY READING CAREFULLY ALL THE INFORMATION SENT BY EACH UNIVERSITY. As you learn more about the application process, however, you will be able to guess which tests a student must take.

Can you guess correctly which tests the following students will probably have to take? Use Figure 3A on page 33 to help you.

1. Jeong Kim will graduate from Seoul National University in Korea with a bachelor's degree in chemistry. He wants to attend a large research university to study for his Ph.D. degree in chemistry. Should he take the GRE subject test?

2. Wei Mei Wong has a bachelor's degree in economics from Hong Kong University. She wants to study for a master's degree in business administration at a large university in Michigan or Ohio. What tests does she need to take?

3. Ali Hamad Al-Kaneeb has been studying English in an intensive English program at a community college in Florida. He completed his secondary studies in Kuwait before coming to the United States. He wants to move to Chicago and attend a community college to begin his pre-engineering studies. Does he need to take the ACT or SAT?

Questions and Answers

What happens if I don't take the tests listed in the information brochure of the university?

Your application may not be considered at all. At some colleges and universities, the scores are necessary before the school can decide whether to admit a student.

When we asked admissions officers what most frequently delays the admission process for international students, many said, "Missing test scores—TOEFL, SAT, GRE, etc. We can't make decisions without the test scores."

If you have problems arranging to take a test, be sure to inform the admissions officer exactly what the problem is.

How do I prepare or study for these tests?

A bulletin (small booklet) is available free from each testing organization. The bulletin includes sample test questions. Practice tests are also available from most testing organizations.

There are also many test-preparation practice books for sale. You may find, however, that the sample questions in the free bulletins are all that you need to get an idea what the test is like.

My friend has an information brochure from a college. It says he has to take a placement test when he arrives on campus. What does that mean?

Placement tests are given *after* a student applies, is accepted, and decides to enroll at a college or university. The tests are usually prepared by the teachers at the college. The scores are used to place students in the correct level of classes. Placement tests are often given to U.S. students to place students in the correct English, mathematics, and foreign language classes. There is no fee for a placement test given by the university.

In addition to placement tests, many universities give international students another English language proficiency test when a student enters the university. The test is used to confirm that a student has sufficient English skills and, if necessary, to place a student in the correct English-as-a-second-language class.

I want to go to a university in September. I plan to take the TOEFL in March, but I'm afraid I'll get a low score. Can I be admitted to the university and study English in the English language program?

Probably not. You must satisfy the requirements with regard to your TOEFL score. Enrolling in the English language program is not the same as being admitted to the university, and neither does it guarantee you admission.

I haven't made plans yet to take the TOEFL. What do I write on my application form?

STOP! If you haven't made plans yet, you shouldn't be filling in the form! Make arrangements immediately! In some places, tests are given only two or three times a year. You must check schedules and arrange to take the test before you send in the application form.

ENGLISH LANGUAGE TESTS

Most universities require international students who have learned English as a second or foreign language to take English tests *before* admission. Undergraduate and graduate applicants must take English tests. Sometimes if a graduate student has had undergraduate studies in certain English-speaking countries, he or she does not have to take an English test.

The TOEFL test is designed to test the general English language abilities of students who have learned English as a second or foreign language. The MELAB is another English language test. An applicant can take either test. Both tests are recognized by most universities as ways to show that a student has sufficient English to be accepted for academic study.

Registering for the TOEFL/TWE/TSE

To take the TOEFL, you need a TOEFL/TSE information bulletin. ETS sends copies of the bulletin to educational organizations around the world. A student can go or write to various educational advising centers, such as United States Information Service (USIS) offices, to get a free bulletin. Figures 3B–3D show some of the important materials you will receive in the bulletin.

Figure 3B.   Where to Obtain a *Bulletin of Information*

If you are located outside the United States and Canada and bulletins are not available at your institution or agency, students may obtain individual copies of the *Bulletin* from United States educational commissions and foundations, United States Information Service (USIS) offices, binational centers, and some private educational organizations. They may also order directly from the representative that serves the area or country in which they plan to take the test.

ALGERIA, BAHRAIN, IRAQ, KUWAIT, OMAN, QATAR, SAUDI ARABIA, SUDAN, UNITED ARAB EMIRATES:
AMIDEAST
Testing Programs, Suite 300
1100 17th Street, NW
Washington, DC 20036-4601, USA

BRAZIL:
Instituto Brasil-Estados Unidos
Av. Nossa Senhora de Copacabana
690-8° Andar
22050 Rio de Janeiro, RJ, Brasil

CANADA:
Information Centre for Canada
P.O. Box 162, Station S
Toronto, ON   M5M 4L7
Canada

EGYPT:
AMIDEAST
6 Kamel El Shennawy Street
Second Floor, Apartment 5
Garden City, Cairo, Egypt
or
AMIDEAST
American Cultural Center
3 Pharaana Street
Azarita, Alexandria
Egypt

EUROPE:
(all countries, including Cyprus, Great Britain, Iceland, and Turkey)
CITO-TOEFL
P.O. Box 1203
6801 BE Arnhem
Netherlands

HONG KONG:
Hong Kong Examinations Authority
San Po Kong Sub-office
17 Tseuk Luk Street
San Po Kong
Kowloon, Hong Kong

INDIA:
Institute of Psychological and
   Educational Measurement
25-A Mahatma Gandhi Marg
Allahabad, U.P. 211 001, India

INDONESIA:
Institute of International Education
P.O. Box 18 KBYCO
Jakarta Selatan 12950, Indonesia

JAPAN:
Council on International
   Educational Exchange
Hirakawa-cho Kaisaka Bldg. 1F
1-6-8 Hirakawa-cho, Chiyoda-ku
Tokyo, 102 Japan

JORDAN:
AMIDEAST
P.O. Box 1249
Amman, Jordan

KOREA:
Korean-American
   Educational Commission
K.P.O. Box 643
Seoul 110-606, Korea

LEBANON:
AMIDEAST
P.O. Box 135-155
Ras Beirut, Lebanon
or
AMIDEAST
P.O. Box 70-744
Antelias, Beirut, Lebanon

MALAYSIA:
MACEE
TOEFL/TSE Services
355, Jalan Ampang
50450 Kuala Lumpur, Malaysia

MEXICO:
Institute of International Education
Londres 16, 2nd Floor
Apartado Postal 61-115
Mexico 06600 D.F., Mexico

MOROCCO:
AMIDEAST
25 bis, Patrice Lumumba
Apt. No. 8
Rabat, Morocco

PEOPLE'S REPUBLIC OF CHINA:
China International Examinations
   Coordination Bureau
#30 Yuquan Road, 100039
Beijing
People's Republic of China

SINGAPORE:
MACEE
TOEFL/TSE Services
355, Jalan Ampang
50450 Kuala Lumpur, Malaysia

SYRIA:
AMIDEAST
P.O. Box 2313
Damascus, Syria

TAIWAN:
The Language Training &
   Testing Center
P.O. Box 23-41
Taipei 10098, Taiwan

THAILAND:
Institute of International Education
Room 219
A.U.A. Language Center
179 Rajadamri Road
G.P.O. Box 2050
Bangkok 10501, Thailand

TUNISIA:
AMIDEAST
BP 1134
Tunis, Tunisia

YEMEN
AMIDEAST
P.O. Box 1088
Sana'a, Yemen

ALL OTHER COUNTRIES AND AREAS:
TOEFL/TSE Publications
P.O. Box 6154
Princeton, NJ 08541-6154, USA

Reprinted by permission of Educational Testing Service, the copyright owner. No endorsement of this publication by Educational Testing Service should be inferred.

Figure 3C. Sample TOEFL/TSE Registration (Application) Form

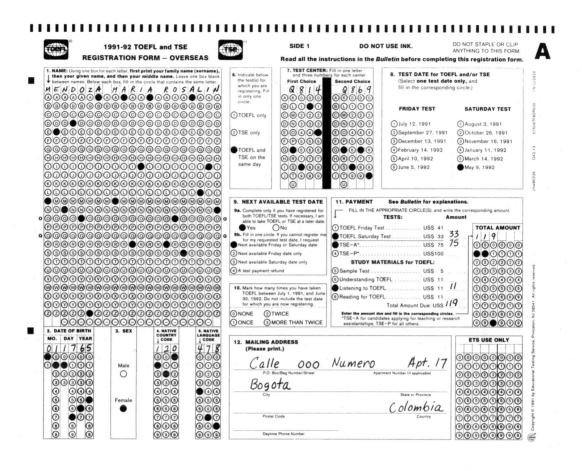

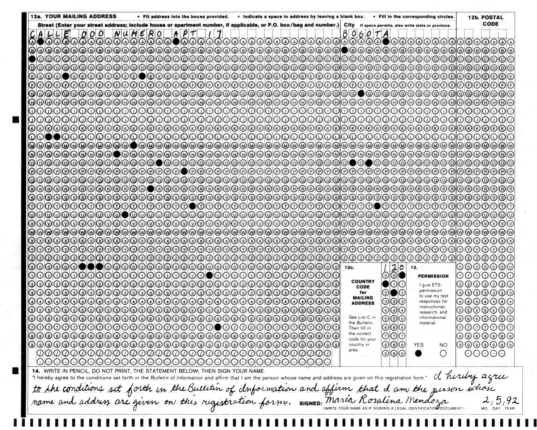

Figure 3D. **Examinee's Portion of TOEFL/TSE Registration Package**

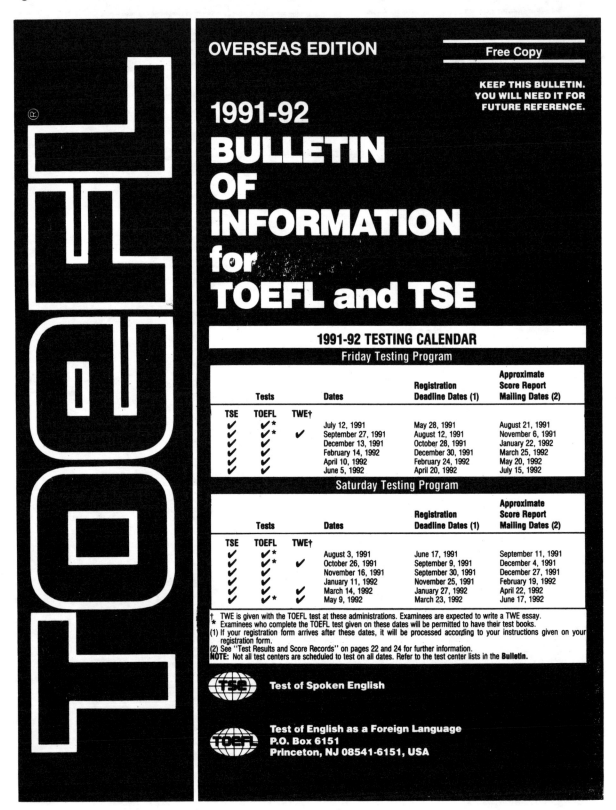

OVERSEAS EDITION

Free Copy

KEEP THIS BULLETIN.
YOU WILL NEED IT FOR
FUTURE REFERENCE.

1991-92
BULLETIN OF INFORMATION for TOEFL and TSE

1991-92 TESTING CALENDAR

Friday Testing Program

Tests			Dates	Registration Deadline Dates (1)	Approximate Score Report Mailing Dates (2)
TSE	TOEFL	TWE†			
✔	✔*		July 12, 1991	May 28, 1991	August 21, 1991
✔	✔*	✔	September 27, 1991	August 12, 1991	November 6, 1991
✔	✔		December 13, 1991	October 28, 1991	January 22, 1992
✔	✔		February 14, 1992	December 30, 1991	March 25, 1992
✔	✔		April 10, 1992	February 24, 1992	May 20, 1992
✔	✔		June 5, 1992	April 20, 1992	July 15, 1992

Saturday Testing Program

Tests			Dates	Registration Deadline Dates (1)	Approximate Score Report Mailing Dates (2)
TSE	TOEFL	TWE†			
✔	✔*		August 3, 1991	June 17, 1991	September 11, 1991
✔	✔*	✔	October 26, 1991	September 9, 1991	December 4, 1991
✔	✔		November 16, 1991	September 30, 1991	December 27, 1991
✔	✔		January 11, 1992	November 25, 1991	February 19, 1992
✔	✔	✔	March 14, 1992	January 27, 1992	April 22, 1992
✔	✔*	✔	May 9, 1992	March 23, 1992	June 17, 1992

† TWE is given with the TOEFL test at these administrations. Examinees are expected to write a TWE essay.
* Examinees who complete the TOEFL test given on these dates will be permitted to have their test books.
(1) If your registration form arrives after these dates, it will be processed according to your instructions given on your registration form.
(2) See "Test Results and Score Records" on pages 22 and 24 for further information.
NOTE: Not all test centers are scheduled to test on all dates. Refer to the test center lists in the **Bulletin.**

Test of Spoken English

Test of English as a Foreign Language
P.O. Box 6151
Princeton, NJ 08541-6151, USA

Some international students get the bulletin from the TOEFL headquarters at ETS in Princeton, New Jersey, in the United States. Other students get a special bulletin prepared for students in their particular country.

In the bulletin there is a registration form. The student fills in the form and then puts the form and the test fee payment in the envelope provided. The envelope has the address where it should be sent printed on the envelope.

The registration form will be read by a computer scanner machine. If a student does not fill in the circles or ovals, the machine cannot read it. Every part of the form must be completed.

Registering for the MELAB

The MELAB (Michigan English Language Assessment Battery) is another English language proficiency test for applicants to U.S. universities. Some universities call it "the Michigan test" and some refer to it by its former name—the MTELP (Michigan Test of English Language Proficiency).

All official MELAB tests are arranged through

English Language Institute
The University of Michigan
3020 North University Building
Ann Arbor, MI 48109-1057 USA

Scores are reported by the ELI–UM (English Language Institute—The University of Michigan) to the universities.

The MELAB is given by examiners in 120 countries. A free information bulletin on the MELAB and the registration application form are available from the ELI–UM.

In China, students can get MELAB application information from

CIECB (China International Examinations Coordination Bureau)
No. 30, Yu Quan Road
Beijing 100039
People's Republic of China

There are no registration deadlines with the MELAB. As soon as a student sends in the application form (test registration form) with the fee and receives authorization to be tested, the test can be arranged with one of the local examiners in his or her country. After the test is given, the test papers are sent back to the ELI–UM in Ann Arbor where the tests are scored. The test scores are usually sent to universities within 14 days of when they are received at Michigan.

The MELAB can be a convenient test for international students who need to take an English proficiency test. Some universities prefer the MELAB because it always includes a written composition.

Practice

EXERCISE 3-5

Look at Figure 3B, the list of places international students get TOEFL/TSE information bulletins. Use Figure 3B to help answer the following questions.

1. Where can you apply for a bulletin?
2. Why should you get a registration bulletin long before you need to take the test?
3. How much money do you pay for a bulletin?

Late scores often hurt the applicant's file and if we never get an English score we will not consider the student unless special circumstances exist.

–Admissions Officer

EXERCISE 3-6

In the TOEFL/TSE bulletin, there is a special registration form. You need to complete this form to register for the test. Look at the sample in Figure 3C. Can you read it?

1. In what section of the form did Maria write her birthdate? What is her birthday?
2. How many tests does she want to take?
3. When does she want to take the tests?
4. How much does each test cost? What else is Maria paying for?
5. What is the country code for Colombia? In what section does Maria write the code?

EXERCISE 3-7

Look at the deadlines in the testing calendar in Figure 3D. Maria completed her form and signed it on February 5. There is a deadline—a last date when she can get the form to the testing organization.

1. What is the date by which the office in New Jersey must receive her registration form?
2. How many weeks before the deadline should she mail her registration form?
3. What do you think will happen if she does not include her payment in the envelope?
4. Maria forgot to complete one part of the form in Figure 3C. Can you find what she forgot to mark?

EXERCISE 3-8

Most universities give information to students about what tests they should take. In the bulletin "Admission Information for International Graduate Applicants" from Ohio State University, we can find a section about English proficiency test requirements.

Read the bulletin excerpt and then write in which paragraphs you can find answers to the questions that follow it.

English Proficiency

Test Requirements

(1) Ohio State requires that all admitted applicants have sufficient knowledge of the English language to follow their proposed program of study. To assure such competence, the University normally requires any applicant whose native language is not English to submit scores from either the Test of English as a Foreign Language (TOEFL) or the Michigan English Language Assessment Battery (MELAB).

(2) Citizens of the following countries are exempt from the TOEFL or MELAB requirement, because these countries are considered native English-speaking: Australia, Belize, the British Caribbean and British West Indies, Canada (except Quebec), England, Guyana, Ireland, Liberia, New Zealand, Scotland, the United States, and Wales. In addition, applicants are exempt if they have received a university degree of bachelor's or higher from a university in one of these countries.

(3) The minimum acceptable TOEFL score is 500; the minimum acceptable MELAB score is 80. Some graduate programs require scores higher than these minimums.

(4) Those applicants required to submit TOEFL or MELAB must do so before they can be admitted. Ohio State does not conditionally admit applicants who have not met the requirement for proof of English proficiency.

(5) It is to the advantage of the applicant to take the TOEFL early in the application process. The TOEFL *Bulletin,* which includes a registration form, is available in many locations outside the United States, usually at American embassies and consulates, offices of the United States Information Agency (USIA), United States educational commissions and foundations, binational centers, and many private organizations, such as the Institute of International Education (IIE), the African-American Institute (AAI), American-Mideast Educational & Training Services (AMIDEAST), and the American-Korean Foundation. You may also write to TOEFL, P.O. Box 6154, Princeton, NJ, 08541-6154, USA.

(6) The Test of Written English will be administered as part of the TOEFL during the October, March, and May administrations of the TOEFL. Students applying for admission to Ohio State are encouraged to register for the TOEFL on one of these test dates. The Test of Written English will allow applicants to demonstrate to University departments and admissions officials their writing proficiency, an important measure of ability to compete in academic work. Details on the Test of Written English are contained in the TOEFL Bulletin.

(7) Applicants may register for the MELAB if they are unable to take TOEFL. For more detailed information about MELAB, contact the English Language Institute, Testing and Certification, University of Michigan, Ann Arbor, Michigan 48104.

(8) As a further evaluation of competence in English, all admitted students whose native language is not English will be required to take a written examination when they arrive at the University before a program of study is officially approved.

(9) Students whose scores on the examination indicate that they need further work to improve their English-writing skills will be required to take one or more special English courses, concurrently with a reduced academic course load. The English-as-a-second language courses cannot be used as credit toward a degree. The international student should realize in advance that deficiencies in English may thus increase the amount of time and money required for completing a regular program of study.

Test of Spoken English Required for Applicants for Teaching Associateship

(10) Those graduate applicants required to submit TOEFL or MELAB who wish to be considered for a teaching associateship must also demonstrate adequate skill in spoken English. Such applicants are therefore required to take the Test of Spoken English (TSE) and to have official scores submitted directly to the Admissions Office. The TSE *Bulletin* and registration form are included in the TOEFL *Bulletin.* Applicants should request complete information about the spoken English requirement from their prospective graduate programs.

The American Language Program

(11) The University has an intensive English program for students who do not pos-

sess the required proficiency in English or who wish to improve their language skills. Separate application must be made for admission to this course of study. For information write to: American Language Program, The Ohio State University, 117A Ohio Stadium East, 1961 Tuttle Park Place, Columbus, Ohio 43210, USA. **Acceptance to the American Language Program does not guarantee subsequent admission to an academic program at OSU.**

1. What extra test is needed if an applicant wants a graduate teaching associateship at Ohio State?
2. What is the lowest TOEFL score generally allowed? the lowest MELAB score?
3. Why would a student want to take the TOEFL in October, March, or May?
4. Who does not need to take the TOEFL or MELAB?
5. What can someone do if his or her scores on the university's written test are too low for admission to regular academic study?
6. What English test must students take after they have been admitted and arrive at Ohio State University?

EXERCISE 3-9

Is it possible? Refer to the admission information in the bulletin excerpt in Exercise 3-8 and explain each situation.

1. Jeong applied to study engineering mechanics at Ohio State. He has a TOEFL score of 525. He received a letter from the university. The letter said his English score did not meet the requirements for admission.
2. Ahmed knows his MELAB score of 74 is too low for regular admission. He wants to study in a graduate chemistry program. He does not understand why he cannot be admitted to study chemistry and take some English language classes to work on his English at the same time.

Questions and Answers

How do I register for the TWE (Test of Written English)?
The TWE is offered as part of the TOEFL four times a year—September, October, March, and May. You do not register for it separately. If the universities that you are applying to recommend that applicants take the TWE, then you should register for the TOEFL in one of the months when the TWE is included in the TOEFL.

I am applying to several schools. Some of them say I should take the TOEFL and some say I can take the TOEFL or MELAB. Should I take both tests?
You probably don't need to take both tests. Most universities will accept either TOEFL or MELAB scores. You should follow the instructions given by the university, however, do not hesitate to write to the admissions officer if you have any questions.

Why do different universities and different programs within one university have different minimum requirements for examination scores? One school says I must have a 560 on the TOEFL, and another says a score of 520 is enough.

Again, remember the structure of U.S. education. Each university and sometimes each department has its own standards. A few of the many possible explanations are

- The individual experience of admissions officials in each university or department
- What kind of English language services the university has available for enrolled students
- The selectivity of the university (A university that gets a lot of applications can choose those with the highest test scores.)
- The English language skills needed for the program the student is applying to.

Some universities are more flexible than others about the lowest scores considered acceptable. If you think your language skills are better than your test score shows, you should probably take the test again.

I don't have enough money for all the university fees and living expenses. I need financial assistance from the university. My friend told me that if I take the TSE the university will give me a teaching assistantship job. If I take the TSE, will I get financial assistance?

It's true that many graduate students receive financial assistance from U.S. universities. Some universities want to know how well you speak English, so they ask you to take the TSE. If you speak English well, you will do well on the TSE, and that may help your chances of receiving a teaching assistantship position. Scores of above 220 on TSE comprehensibility are generally considered adequate scores. Your test scores cannot, however, guarantee you a financial award. Many universities have their own tests for screening students for teaching positions. These tests are taken after you have been accepted as a student and arrive on campus.

UNDERGRADUATE APPLICANTS— ACADEMIC TESTS

Most four-year universities require that freshman applicants take an academic entrance test, either the SAT or the ACT.

Universities that have many applicants offer admission to the best students who apply. They select those students with the best academic abilities. They use SAT or ACT scores to help them decide which students have the best academic abilities. The information a university sends to applicants gives facts about the kind of students usually chosen to attend there and the importance of SAT or ACT scores in admissions decisions.

An applicant does *not* need to take both the ACT and SAT. An applicant usually takes one test or the other. Most universities that require international applicants to take an academic entrance test will accept scores on either the ACT or SAT.

The ACT (American College Testing Program)

The ACT test is an admission test designed to evaluate American students who are native speakers of English and who are going to be university freshmen. It is produced by the ACT Program, which has its main offices in Iowa City, Iowa.

The ACT is given four times a year—usually in October, December, February, and April. (The exact dates differ from year to year.) In some countries the ACT is given only one, two, or three times a year.

All the information about registering for the ACT is available in a free booklet, "Taking the ACT Assessment for Students outside the U.S.," which is available from

ACT Operations
P.O. Box 808
Iowa City, Iowa 52243
USA

The SAT (Scholastic Aptitude Test)

The SAT is an admission test produced by the College Board ATP (Admissions Testing Program) of ETS (Educational Testing Service), which has its main offices in Princeton, New Jersey.

The SAT serves the same purposes for universities as the ACT: it is designed to evaluate American students who are native speakers of English and who are going to be university freshmen. If a university wants an international student to take the SAT, the college will list it as a requirement of admission.

The SAT is given six times a year in some countries. In some countries it is given only once, twice, three times, or four times a year.

All the information about registering for the SAT is available in a free registration bulletin—"SAT and Achievement Tests." To test outside the United States, students use the international edition of the registration bulletin. The international bulletin is available from

College Board ATP
P.O. Box 6200
Princeton, NJ 08541-6200
USA

The SAT registration bulletin gives all the information you need about registering for the test. The College Board also produces two other free bulletins—"Taking the SAT" and "Taking the Achievement Tests." Copies of these booklets are sent each year to secondary schools. You can write to the College Board ATP address in Princeton, New Jersey, about where you can get copies of these two booklets. The booklets contain sample questions and scoring information.

When a student takes the SAT, he or she gets two scores, a *verbal* score and a *mathematical* score. The scores are reported on a scale from 200 (low) to 800 (high). The average (mean) score of all students who take the SAT is about 425 on each. The average score for U.S. high school seniors who are going on to college is higher—about 475.

Some universities base admissions decisions on a combination of the verbal and mathematical scores. A selective university might want applicants to have a total score of 1100 or higher.

Admissions officers will take into account the fact that the verbal section can be difficult for nonnative speakers of English. In fact, one of the reasons you should also take the TOEFL is to help admissions officers interpret a low verbal score.

Some selective universities that require the SAT of freshman applicants also require applicants to take special supplementary tests, called *achievement tests,* in from one to three subjects, such as biology or U.S. history or social studies. Achievement tests are intended to measure knowledge of specific school subjects.

Practice

EXERCISE 3-10

A profile is a brief description. Profiles of a university and its students are included in university information brochures.

Read the information from a profile about Bucknell University and answer the questions that follow it. Bucknell University is in Pennsylvania. The total enrollment is about 3500. Each year about 850 freshmen are admitted. The profile helps students decide whether they should apply to Bucknell.

Admission

Bucknell is highly selective and admission is competitive. Credentials required include a written personal essay on the application form, transcript of high school record, recommendations from counselors and teachers, and the results of the College Board SAT. Students for whom English is not their first language are expected to submit the results of the Test of English as a Foreign Language (TOEFL) to show English proficiency. The minimum TOEFL score is 550.

Applications for regular admission must be filed by January 1 for U.S. citizens; February 2 for foreign students; for early decision by December 1. Early decisions are announced by January 1; all other decisions are announced before April 1.

Unfortunately, because there is no financial aid available at Bucknell for non-U.S. citizens, all applicants who require financial assistance must acquire funding from outside sources.

Entrance Examinations. As an applicant, you are required to take the Scholastic Aptitude Test (SAT) of the College Board or the American College Test (ACT) prior to January of your senior year. (The results of the SAT or ACT tests taken in March of the senior year are received too late to be considered by the Admissions Committee.)

Bucknell no longer requires the English and Mathematic Achievement Tests as a requirement related to enrollment at Bucknell. Bucknell does require the Foreign Language Achievement Test of any student planning to enroll in foreign language study at Bucknell.

To obtain an application form for College Board tests and a schedule for test dates and locations, write directly to the College Entrance Examination Board, Box 592, Princeton, New Jersey 08540.

Typical Profile. In recent years, Bucknell has received an average of 6,600 applications for a freshman class of 850. Of those students admitted, approximately 60 percent ranked in the top tenth, and 80 percent ranked in the top fifth of their high-school graduating class.

The mean SAT scores for recent classes have been 558 verbal and 636 mathematic. These figures cannot be used to predict chances of an individual acceptance by Bucknell, since high-school SAT scores or rank in class alone will not guarantee admission, nor will scores slightly below these figures automatically disqualify an applicant.

Foreign Students. Bucknell welcomes applications from foreign students who have outstanding secondary school records and who meet the entrance requirements of the University.

Application forms and instructions are available from the Admissions Office. Foreign applications should be filed early in the year for September entrance, and all credentials must arrive in the Admissions Office prior to March 1 of the year of admission.

The two primary points of consideration are the student's academic preparation and fluency in English. In addition to the application form, the following should be submitted to the Office of Admissions: 1) the results of the Test of English as a Foreign Language (TOEFL), the SAT, or the ACT; 2) official copies of the student's secondary school record and university records if applicable (documents in languages other than English must accompanied by complete and literal translation into English); 3) two character and two academic references, to be sent directly to Bucknell; and 4) certification of arrangements for financing the entire four years.

Students offered admission will be required to complete a medical form which will be sent with the registration material.

Important Deadlines.

December 1 – The deadline by which early decision application must be submitted.

December 20 – Announcement of all early decisions.

January 1 – The deadline for regular applications.

April 1 – The date by which all admissions decisions are announced.

May 1 – The required response date or candidates reply date for students offered admission. A $200 deposit is required to confirm enrollment intentions.

1. What are the average SAT verbal and mathematical scores of students who apply to Bucknell?

2. A score of 438 is _____ below the average mathematical score of all Bucknell applicants.

   a. slightly   b. extremely

3. A score of 540 is _____ below the average verbal score.

   a. slightly   b. extremely

4. "These figures cannot be used..." "Figures" refers to

   a. number of applications   b. SAT scores   c. rank in school

EXERCISE 3-11

The standards for admission of U.S. and international applicants are different. An applicant should read carefully *all* the information sent by the university. Special attention should be given to the directions to international students. Some information is in the information brochure, some on the application form.

Read the excerpts from Bucknell's information to students from Exercise 3-10.

1. How are the entrance tests different for U.S. and international applicants?

2. What tests should a freshman international applicant take?

3. A student who wants to enter Bucknell in September 1993 should plan to take the TOEFL on or before

   a. November 1992   b. January 1993   c. March 1993   d. June 1993

EXERCISE 3-12

Read the instructions from the ACT information booklet. Then put the following list in the proper order. What should be done first, second, and so on?

Arranging to Take the Test

- If any of the special circumstances listed below apply to you, **read and follow the special instructions.**
- Select a test date from the schedule on page 1 to take the ACT Assessment.
- Select a test center from the list of ACT test centers beginning on page 4. Be sure the center is scheduled to administer the ACT Assessment on the date you have chosen.
- Contact the test center supervisor using the telephone number or address given in the list, on or before the registration deadline for the test date you have chosen. If you write to the test center, be sure to include your full name, address, and telephone number. The test center supervisor will tell you where you will be taking the examination (building, room number, etc.). In the space provided on your packet envelope, write the **exact** location to which you are to report on the test date.

- If you find you must make a change in your plans to test on a certain date, be sure to write or call your test center supervisor as soon as possible.
- Complete pages 1, 2, and 4 of the answer folder (see instructions below). Do not return the answer folder to ACT.
- If you do not have current photo identification, ask your counselor for a school letter of identification (see page 24).
- Obtain a check or money order drawn on a bank in the United States for the correct fee. Contact your local bank to make arrangements to obtain U.S. funds **drawn on a bank in the United States.** Do NOT bring cash.
- Report to your test center by 8:00 A.M. on the date you are scheduled to test.
- **You will not be admitted to test without acceptable identification.**
- Keep this booklet for reference. It includes information about the test day and how to request additional score reports after you take the test.

Used with permission of ACT—The American College Testing Program.

a. Contact the test supervisor in your country at least a week before the test date to get the exact test location.

b. Go at 8 o'clock in the morning on the day of the test to the test center and take with you your answer folder, your check for the test fees, proper photo identification, and pencils with erasers.

c. Write to ACT in Iowa, USA, for the test registration packet for international students.

d. Answer the questions about yourself on the ACT answer folder on pages 1, 2, and 4.

e. Choose a test date and test center from the list in the ACT booklet.

f. Get a check for the amount of test fees drawn on a U.S. bank.

EXERCISE 3-13

The registration bulletin provides a lot of information. Look at the contents of the bulletin from another test, the SAT in Figure 3E. On what page might you find the following information?

1. How to fill in the registration form
2. The 4-number code for the colleges you want to receive your scores
3. The dates the test is given in your country
4. How to get the scores to a college more quickly
5. How you can take the test if it's too late to register
6. What to do if you do not have enough money to pay for the test fees

Figure 3E.   Excerpts from the SAT Bulletin

A

CONTENTS

2 About the Tests	6 Changing Your Test Choice,	10 Canceling Your Scores
2 SAT/TSWE	Test Date, or Test Center	10 Archived Scores
2 Achievement Tests	7 On the Test Day	10 Missing Scores
3 Plan Ahead	7 Acceptable Identification	10 SAT Question-and-Answer
3 Do You Have the Right Bulletin?	7 Taking the Test	Service
3 If You Need Help	7 Questioning a Test Question	10 SAT Score Verification Service
4 Completing the Registration Form	8 Complaints about the Test Center	11 Student Descriptive Questionnaire
4 Student Search Service	8 Absence from a Test	(SDQ)
5 Special Registration Situations	8 Score Reporting	15 College Majors by Academic Area
5 Fee Waivers	8 Score Reports	of Study
5 Late Registration	8 Sending Additional Reports:	16 Special Information for Students
5 Testing as a Standby	Additional Report Request Form	Testing Outside the United States
5 Sunday Administrations	9 Telephone Rush Reporting Service	18 Test Centers and Codes
5 Students Requiring a	9 Stopping Automatic Reporting	23 Country Codes
Sign Language Interpreter	of Scores	24 College and Scholarship Program
5 Students with Disabilities	9 Cancellation of Scores by the	Codes
6 Admission Ticket/Correction Form	College Board	32 1990-91 Test Dates and Fees

THE COLLEGE BOARD

Keep this Bulletin for future reference. You may need it even after you have taken the test, particularly if you register for another test or want to have scores sent to additional colleges and scholarship programs.

B

1990-91 International Test Dates[1] (SAT and Achievement Tests cannot be taken on the same day.)		Postmark date for regular registration (See Testing as a Standby, page 5.)	Receipt date for special requests[2]
November 3[3]	SAT & Ach[4]	September 24	September 5
December 1	SAT & Ach[4]	October 22	October 3
January 26[3]	SAT & Ach[4]	December 17	November 28
March 16[3]	SAT only	February 4	January 16
May 4[3]	SAT & Ach[4]	March 25	March 6
June 1	SAT & Ach[4]	April 22	April 3

[1] For Sunday administrations, see page 5.
[2] Requests for special testing arrangements (see page 16) must be *received* by the special requests deadline.
[3] The SAT Question-and-Answer Service is available only for November 3, January 26, March 16, May 4, and May 5 test dates. (See page 10.)
[4] A full schedule of Achievement Test dates is on the inside front cover.

Reprinted by permission of the College Entrance Examination Board. Permission to reprint the SAT material does not constitute review or endorsement by the College Board of this publication.

EXERCISE 3-14

Look at the chart of international SAT test dates in Figure 3E. (Special request arrangements might be made if you live more than 75 miles from a test center or cannot for religious reasons take the test on a Saturday.) Choose the best answer.

1. Suki wanted her SAT scores to arrive at a college by December 1. She should have taken the SAT _____.

2. Jean-Paul wanted to take the SAT in November. He should have written to the College Board for an SAT registration bulletin by _____.

3. Kouleer lives 200 miles from the nearest SAT testing center. He would like to take the test closer to his hometown. He wants to take the test in May. He should send in his registration with a letter explaining his situation to the College Board before _____.

Questions and Answers

I can't take the SAT or ACT where I live. What should I do?

Take an English proficiency test—the TOEFL or MELAB. If your scores are high and you have a strong academic background, you may not need an academic test score. Universities are often flexible and will consider some international freshman applicants without SAT or ACT scores.

What will happen if I take the tests late?

DON'T DELAY IN TAKING TESTS. You will seriously harm your chances for admission if your test scores are not in your file. Remember it takes about six weeks after you take the test for the scores to reach the university!

There is a question about educational opportunities in the student profile section of the ACT answer folder. If I mark "yes," does that mean I will get a scholarship?

No, it only means that you give permission to the ACT program to give information about you to universities that may be looking for students. If you do receive information from a university to which you did not write yourself, you can read the information. If you decide to apply to the university, you apply just as you would to any university. It does not mean you will get a scholarship from that university.

What is one of the most common problems in taking the SAT or ACT?

Admissions officers say **"Make sure your name is spelled correctly.** We get the test scores on a computer tape, and we can never find the score if the name is wrong!!"

SPELL YOUR NAME THE SAME WAY ON EVERYTHING—TESTS AND ADMISSION FORMS.

GRADUATE APPLICANTS—ACADEMIC TESTS AND SPECIAL ENGLISH TESTS

The GRE (Graduate Record Examinations) and Subject Tests

Applicants to graduate programs also are often required to take academic entrance tests. The most common test is the Graduate Record Examination (GRE). The GRE General Test contains sections to measure verbal, quantitative, and analytical skills. The test is designed for U.S. students who are native speakers of English.

In addition to the GRE General Test, some university graduate departments want applicants to take one or more GRE Subject Tests. The GRE Subject Tests are designed to test the knowledge a student learned about various subjects as an undergraduate student. GRE Subject Tests cover 16 subjects:

Biochemistry, Cell and Molecular Biology	Economics	Mathematics
	Education	Music
	Engineering	Physics
Biology	Geology	Political Science
Chemistry	History	Psychology
Computer Science	Literature in English	Sociology

A GRE Subject Test is taken in the afternoon. A subject test takes about three hours. A student cannot take two subject tests in the same afternoon. (No subject tests are ever given on June GRE test dates.)

A GRE General Test can be taken on one test date and a GRE Subject Test on another test date, but a student must register two times—once for each test date.

Many international students register for GRE Tests through ETS (Educational Testing Service) in the United States but take the tests in their own country. Information on registration for GRE Tests (General and Subject Tests), a practice General Test, and a description of the content of Subject Tests is available in the GRE information bulletin published by the ETS. Write

Graduate Record Examinations
Educational Testing Service
P.O. Box 6000
Princeton, NJ 08541-6000
USA

International students in some countries must register through a GRE registration agent in their country. The agents have test information bulletins, too.

The GMAT (Graduate Management Admissions Test)

The GMAT is a special test designed to test applicants to graduate business studies programs. It is similar to the GRE, but the content of the test is more directed to business topics. The multiple-choice test has verbal sections and sections that focus on measuring quantitative (mathematical) abilities. The test is produced by the ETS (Educational Testing Service). The test is designed for native speakers of English. The verbal sections are considered especially difficult for some nonnative speakers.

Most graduate business programs prefer that applicants take the GMAT. Some will accept either GMAT or GRE scores.

English Language Tests and Graduate Student Financial Awards

Universities sometimes use English language test scores to help them decide which graduate students can be offered financial awards. One kind of financial award is a teaching fellowship or assistantship award.

Some universities require that applicants who want teaching positions take the TSE (Test of Spoken English). The TSE gives department admissions officers more information about an applicant's ability to speak English.

Some universities look at the TOEFL score and only offer teaching awards to those with the highest scores—560 at some universities and, sometimes, above 600 at other universities.

Most universities that offer teaching assistantship awards have additional English language tests that the student takes upon arrival at the university.

The amount of money and other benefits (reduced tuition fees, health insurance, etc.) that a graduate student receives with such an award varies from university to university and from department to department within the same university.

The graduate student who receives a teaching assistantship award has teaching responsibilities at the U.S. university. A teaching assistant must speak English well to communicate with his or her students.

Practice

EXERCISE 3-15

Read the information on English proficiency from a graduate school of a large university on the next page. Some information is for all international applicants, and some information is specifically for those applicants who would like financial assistance or an award of a teaching assistantship. Based on the information, decide if the assumptions here and on the next page are true or false.

1. Applicants with degrees from U.S. colleges or universities do not have to take an English test.

2. This university accepts MELAB or TOEFL scores as proof of English proficiency.

3. An applicant should take both the TOEFL and MELAB.

ENGLISH PROFICIENCY

As a reflection of the importance the Graduate School places on the ability of its students to communicate effectively, admission will be conditional, for all applicants whose native language is not English, pending their demonstration of English proficiency sufficient to begin graduate-level work here. Those applicants who have received degrees from accredited U.S. institutions will be asked to have their English evaluated when they arrive on campus, prior to the beginning of the term of admission. Applicants whose previous degree is NOT from an accredited U.S. institution, or from an accredited U.S. institution where the majority of instruction is NOT in English will be required to provide score reports from either the Michigan English Language Assessment Battery (MELAB) or the Test of English as a Foreign Language (TOEFL). Information and applications may be obtained by writing to the following:

TOEFL
Educational Testing Service
P.O. Box 6151
Princeton, NJ 08541-6151
U.S.A.

MELAB
English Language Institute
Testing and Certification
3020 NUBS
The University of Michigan
Ann Arbor, MI 48109-1057,
U.S.A.

Generally speaking, if you are applying to the Biological and Physical Sciences or to Engineering programs you will need a minimum total score of 80 on MELAB and 560 on TOEFL. If you are applying to programs in the Social Sciences or in the Humanities and the Arts you will need to have minimum scores of 85 on MELAB or 600 on TOEFL. The School of Music accepts only MELAB scores with a minimum of 83. Asian Studies: China and Japan also accept only MELAB with a minimum score of 88. Only official score reports from TOEFL or MELAB are acceptable. Photocopies will not be considered as official. Score reports should be sent directly to the Graduate School, not to your department.

PLEASE NOTE that re-evaluation of your English proficiency is required on campus before you register if:
(1) your total TOEFL score is 600 or below, or individual sections of the TOEFL are 60 or below;
(2) your Test of Written English (TWE) is 4 or below or missing; or
(3) your total MELAB score is 85 or below, or individual sections of the MELAB are 85 or below.

SOME POINTS TO REMEMBER

- Only official copies of the TOEFL or MELAB score reports are acceptable. Photocopies are not official. Request that your score reports be sent directly to the Graduate School.
- If your native language is not English, some departments/programs will require you to have your English proficiency re-evaluated regardless of your test scores or of the fact that you may have earned a degree from a U.S. or other English-speaking university.
- If you are required, as a condition of your admission, to have your English re-evaluated, you cannot register for academic courses until this has been taken care of. We advise that you arrive in Ann Arbor in plenty of time to have the re-evaluation done before classes start.
- Academic English Evaluation (AEE) is conducted at the English Language Institute just prior to the beginning of each term. The AEE includes measures of writing, listening, speaking, and reading. Students will be counseled individually about their need for courses in English.
- We strongly advise those applicants seeking financial assistance to take the MELAB, including the oral rating section. MELAB examines more areas of English than does TOEFL. Strong scores on the test may enhance your consideration for support.
- Some departments/programs have very specific TOEFL or MELAB score requirements. Contact your department directly for information.
- All international students who have been offered Teaching Assistantships in the College of Literature, Science and Arts or in the College of Engineering are required to have their English skills evaluated to assure competence to teach in the classroom. The evaluation is conducted jointly by the English Language Institute and the department in which the student will be a Teaching Assistant.

4. The psychology program requires higher test scores for admittance than the chemistry program.
5. Photocopies of test reports can be submitted.
6. Test score reports should be sent to the graduate department to which the student is applying.
7. A student who has not taken the TWE must take the campus test when he or she arrives at the university.
8. A student may not register for courses until after he or she has taken the English evaluation.
9. An applicant's chances for financial support at this university are improved if he or she takes the MELAB rather than the TOEFL.
10. After a student takes the Academic English Evaluation, he or she will be given courses to teach.
11. A student who wants a teaching assistantship job must pass another test.
12. A student who wants financial support must have scored above 600 on the TOEFL or 85 on the MELAB.

Questions and Answers

The information I received from the universities says that I must take the GRE. Does that mean the General Test or the Subject Test?

If it just says "GRE," that means the General Test.

How high a GRE score do I need? It just says in the information bulletin from the university that I need to take the GRE. It does not give a minimum score.

It depends on the department and the university. You get three test scores on the GRE General Test—one score for each section. The average score for all students who take the GRE is about 475 on the verbal, 540 on the math, and 500 on the analytical. The verbal section is usually quite difficult for nonnative speakers of English, and departments will overlook a low verbal score (for example, a score of 300—in about the lower 20 percent of all who take the GRE).

The university information states that I must take the GRE. Do I have to take the TOEFL, too?

Probably yes. Read everything the university sends you. The English proficiency requirement will be listed on another page of the information bulletin. All U.S. universities require some proof of English language proficiency.

I have not taken the TOEFL yet, so I do not know whether my score is high enough to apply. What should I do?

It is sometimes difficult for students to judge their own language abilities. Fewer than 10 percent of all students who take the TOEFL achieve a score of 600. Talk to your English teachers about whether you have sufficient language abilities to get an acceptable score.

Also, some U.S. universities have special English programs in the summer for incoming students. Students with borderline admission scores on English tests are sometimes accepted and then strongly encouraged to attend a special English language course in the United States before beginning their academic courses. There are summer English language courses specifically designed for incoming business students. These courses are useful also for students who do have high English test scores but have had few opportunities to use English for daily communication.

What happens if the university awards me a teaching assistantship, but I arrive at the university and do not pass the oral test?

Universities with many teaching assistantship positions usually have special training programs to improve students' general cultural, language, and teaching skills. Most universities that offer a financial award will support a student in another way (with a research position or special fellowship) if a student's communication skills are discovered at the last minute to be lacking.

Courtesy of The University of Iowa

What Are These Application Instructions and Forms Telling Me?

► **APPLICATION INSTRUCTIONS AND FORMS**

► **GRADUATE APPLICATIONS**

► **AREAS OF STUDY**

► **BEGIN AT THE BEGINNING, BUT...**

APPLICATION INSTRUCTIONS AND FORMS

Your application to a university will be the first of many forms you will have to fill in—so, it's a good idea to have some techniques for dealing with forms. **Make a copy of the forms** or, **when you fill them in, use a pencil.** It's easy to make a mistake, and admissions officers don't like reading messy, illegible forms.

Read through the forms before you begin. One reason it's easy to make mistakes is that people expect all forms to be the same and don't read them first. Many forms look the same, but contain important differences.

Read the instructions! All forms have instructions. The instructions are often in small print and may look complicated, but they contain important information. Instructions can give information on

- Eligibility—whether you are qualified to apply
- What they do with the information you give
- Step-by-step advice on answering the questions
- Course names and code numbers

Use the forms. Universities want you to give the information they ask for in the spaces provided on the forms. Admissions officers do not want to worry about attached pages getting lost. It is also frustrating for the university to have to photocopy a lot of extra pages as they process your application. Attach extra pages to your application only when absolutely necessary.

I wish students would read the instructions.

–Admissions Officer

Practice

EXERCISE 4-1

Read the excerpts from the information packets sent by two U.S. universities. Match the words underlined in the excerpts with the explanations given below. Write the word or words on the line after the correct explanation. The first one is done for you as an example.

A Academic System

Level. U.S. citizens normally enter Indiana University after 12 years of elementary and secondary schooling that begins at age 6. Pre-elementary schooling is excluded from this total. *Applicants from other countries should have similar academic backgrounds.* In particular, mathematics and science subjects should have been studied at the secondary level. Secondary level means grades 9-12 inclusive.

The Bachelor's Degree. The first four years of university study are usually spent working toward an undergraduate degree, the bachelor's. A student may attend summer sessions and complete the degree in less time. Several types of bachelor's degrees may be earned depending upon area of study and depth of specialization. All bachelor's degrees include general education in the sciences, social sciences, arts, and humanities, and a field of specialization called the major subject. The major is often combined with one or two related areas of study called minors. Together they form the student's field of concentration.

B 1. Who May Apply

a. Persons with at least a bachelor's degree or the equivalent from an accredited college in the United States or a recognized institution of higher learning abroad. Indian applicants with an arts, science, or commerce degree must present the U.S. bachelor's degree equivalent, i.e., a B.A. and M.A., a B.Sc. and M.Sc., or B.Com. and M.Com. respectively. Furthermore, a grade-point average of 4.0 (A = 5.0) for the last 60 semester hours (or last two years) of undergraduate study is a minimum requirement for admission. In other systems, a 4.0 average is considered the approximate equivalent of a "Very Good," a "Second Class, Upper Division" (from British systems), or a "First Class or Division" (from India, Pakistan, or Bangladesh) et al.

b. Persons who are enrolled in a bachelor's degree program and who are in their senior or final year.

c. Persons who were previously enrolled in the Graduate College on this campus and have broken their pattern of enrollment.

1. Courses given in June, July, and August when
   most students are on vacation: <u>summer sessions</u>

2. Taking courses: _____

3. Similar, almost the same as: _____

4. Inspected to check the quality of teaching: _____

5. Almost a correct estimate: _____

6. Period of study, usually 14–16 weeks: _____

7. Left the university for a while, "dropped out": _____

EXERCISE 4-2

Read the excerpts in Exercise 4-1 carefully and answer the following questions.

1. Does "Academic System" discuss undergraduate or graduate studies?
2. How old are students when they go to the university?
3. Do you include kindergarten (pre-elementary school) when writing about your education?
4. At age six, what grade are U.S. students in?
5. Is it necessary to have studied mathematics and science?
6. In grades 9–12, how old are the students?
7. How long does it take to get a bachelor's?
8. What is a "major"?
9. What subjects do all undergraduates study?
10. What is a "minor"?

EXERCISE 4-3

Refer to the section "Who May Apply" in Exercise 4-1 and answer *True* or *False*.

1. You must have a B.A.
2. A graduate applicant from India must have both a B.A. and an M.A. if applying for a master's program.
3. You can apply in your final year as an undergraduate.
4. A Second Class, Upper Division is less than the equivalent of a 4.0 GPA.
5. You need a degree.

Questions and Answers

There were strikes in my country, so I don't have twelve years of primary and secondary education. Can I still apply?

If your TOEFL or MELAB scores are good, some universities may admit you. It's a good idea to write a letter explaining the situation and giving details of how you continued your studies in those circumstances and what exactly you studied. A letter of recommendation from a teacher or tutor would probably help.

GRADUATE APPLICATIONS

Some universities have a special application form for graduate students. In many ways it is often very similar to the undergraduate form—the same basic information is needed. The educational experience and work sections, however, are different. Experience is often very relevant to graduate students' admission.

Graduate students are expected to have a clear idea of what they are going to study—the field and the level. You may need to discuss with your professors whether you should apply for a master's or doctorate in the United States. In your application you must explain your academic work clearly, so that the admissions officers and the faculty can understand what you have accomplished so far. They will look at your description of the courses you have taken (the time spent, the degree of specialization, the depth of study) to see how the work compares to similar courses offered at their university. They will also look at your grades, your GRE scores, and your letters of recommendation. They want to know how you will fit into their program and contribute to the field.

For graduate applicants, your research experience, awards, and publications are important. You must account for all time—if you took a long vacation for six months, you must put it on your form. The admissions officers will be looking for "gaps"—unexplained periods of time. They want to know how serious you are about your academic career.

You may have to explain any special circumstances, for example, if you worked voluntarily (unpaid) on a project for a professor or if you audited a course (attended classes and did the assignments but didn't register or pay for the courses). In these circumstances, you will need "evidence" of your work—a letter from the professor on letterhead (university stationery), saying exactly what you did and how well you did it.

It helps to write such a summary of your work yourself. Then you have it ready to give to the professor as a memory aid when you request the special letter.

Practice

EXERCISE 4-4

Read this excerpt from the instructions that accompany a graduate application form. The instructions give the general requirements for graduate work.

(a) **The Master's Degree.** Students who have excelled at the undergraduate level may wish to further their study through graduate work. Generally, application to a graduate or professional school is made after receiving the bachelor's degree or during the final year of undergraduate study.

(b) Students entering graduate school often study the same subject that they majored in as undergraduates. Students who choose a new major subject may be required to complete undergraduate courses in that subject without graduate credit to make up deficiencies in background.

(c) The master's degree requires a minimum of one calendar year for completion, but is generally completed within two years. Please note: the M.B.A. and M.P.A. degree programs require a minimum of four semesters of study.

(d) **The Doctorate Degree.** The doctorate is the highest degree awarded in the United States. The doctoral program includes original re-search, course work, a comprehensive examination, and a dissertation. A minimum of three years of study is required beyond the master's level. Few students, however, complete the doctoral degree in three years because of these exacting requirements.

(e) **Special or Nondegree Status.** Students are admitted as special students or in nondegree status for various reasons. Acceptance with such status does not imply that the applicant will later be admitted into a degree program. The credits earned as a special student do not automatically count toward degree requirements should the student be admitted to a degree program at a later date. Students may remain in nondegree status no longer than one year.

(f) **Professional Schools.** Several professional programs are available at Indiana University. All lead to regular degrees (i.e., bachelor's, master's, doctorate) except for the four programs listed below, which have different entry or completion requirements.

The numbered items are summaries of the excerpt written in simple English. Read each summary, then write the letter of the paragraph where you find the information.

1. When to apply for a master's
2. Why? To continue working in your field of study
3. When? During your final year of the bachelor's or after receiving it
4. How long? It takes at least 12 months, usually 2 years
5. Requirements? Excellent undergraduate work
6. What happens when you change your field of study, for example, from math to physics?
7. How long does a doctorate take? At least 3 years, generally more
8. What do I have to do? Research, course work, exams, dissertation
9. The meaning of applying as a special student: you are not automatically admitted to a degree program, you may not be able to use the credits for a degree if you decide to do so later, you can be a special student only for one year
10. The programs in professional schools: they offer bachelor's, master's, doctorates; they have special requirements

Questions and Answers

I'm applying to graduate school and my grades in my major are high, but I have a low TOEFL score. What can I do?

If you have time, study and take the TOEFL again. If the department is impressed with your academic work, they may recommend that you take a summer English course to improve your level before you start taking regular classes. If your English is poor, you will be unable to do your best academic work, and your grades will be low.

AREAS OF STUDY

In the United States, students choose their major areas of study. With your application form you generally get a brochure that lists the degree courses offered. A few courses may not be open to international students; for example, some medical programs for which the number of U.S. students far exceeds the places available. Read the small print carefully.

Practice

EXERCISE 4-5

Figure 4A on page 63 lists undergraduate programs for international students at two universities, University A and University B. For each program, write *A* if it is offered by University A, *B* if by University B, or *Both* if by both.

1. French
2. Portuguese
3. Statistics
4. Microbiology
5. Manufacturing administration
6. Occupational therapy
7. Linguistics

Questions and Answers

I'm interested in specializing in mathematics. Is B (Figure 4A) a better university?

In the excerpt you can see that B has more specialized courses in the field of mathematics. However, the range of courses is only one indication of the quality of a program. The best way to find out about the programs is to talk to an educational counselor or someone who has studied in that field at that university.

I can't decide whether to study mathematics in the College of Liberal Arts or electrical engineering in the College of Engineering. Can I apply to both?

Yes, but you may need to fill in application forms for each college, even though they are at the same university. You may, however, only have to pay one fee. Read the instructions carefully to see if you need to pay twice.

BEGIN AT THE BEGINNING, BUT...

When you receive the application forms from different universities, the first thing you must do is to read them from beginning to end!

Every form may ask for the same information—but each may ask for it in a different way and in a different place.

They ask for too many details. It took me a long time to fill in the form. I needed help with the first ones, then I understood.–*Student*

A clear, neat, well-organized application form creates a good impression. An application form with a lot of mistakes and corrections gives the

Figure 4A.   Undergraduate Programs

A

Levels Available

Program	Bachelor	Master	Specialist	Doctorate
History	✓	✓		
Health Studies (registered health professionals only)	✓			
Home Economics		✓		
Industrial Design	✓ *			
Industrial Education (teaching)	✓			
Interior Design	✓			
Languages (French, German, Latin, Spanish, Latvian)	✓			
Linguistics	✓			
Manufacturing Administration	✓ *	✓		
Mathematics	✓	✓		■
Statistics	✓	✓		
Medieval Studies		✓		
Music	✓	✓		
Occupational Therapy	✓ *	✓		
Operations Research		✓		
Paper Science	✓ *	✓ (GRE)		
Petroleum Distribution	✓			
Philosophy	✓			
Physical Education	✓	✓		
Health Education, Coaching, Elementary/Secondary, Recreation	✓			
Physicians' Assistants	✓			
Physics	✓	✓		
Political Science	✓	✓		
Pre-Professional (Law, Dentistry, Medicine)	✓			
Printing	✓			
Production Technology	✓			
Psychology	✓	✓ (GRE)		■
School Psychology			✓ (GRE)	
Public Administration	✓			

B

LIBERAL ARTS AND SCIENCES

	B	M	D
Foreign languages			
French	•	•	•
German	•	•	•
Greek		•	
Italian	•	•	•
Latin	•	•	
Portuguese	•	•	•
Russian	•		
Spanish	•	•	•
Slavic languages and literatures	•	•	•
Teacher education in French	•	•	
Teacher education in German	•	•	
Teacher education in Latin	•	•	
Teacher education in Russian	•	•	
Teacher education in Spanish	•	•	
Teaching of English as a second language		•	
Health and medical professions[6]			
Medical dietetics	6		
Medical laboratory sciences	6		
Medical record administration	6		
Occupational therapy	6		
Predentistry	6		
Prepharmacy	6		
Pre-physical therapy	6		
Preprofessional nursing	6		
Humanities			
Classical philology			•
Classics	•	•	
Comparative literature	•	•	•
English	•	•	•
Humanities	•		
Library science		•	•
Linguistics	•	•	•
Music	•		
Philosophy	•	•	•
Religious studies	•		
Rhetoric	•		
Speech and hearing science I	7	7	
Speech and hearing science II	8	8	8
Speech communication	•	•	•
Teacher education in speech	•		
Mathematics			
Actuarial science	•		
Mathematics	•	•	•
Mathematics and computer science	•		
Statistics	•	•	•
Teacher education in mathematics	•		
Science			
Anatomical Sciences	•		•
Astronomy	•	•	•
Atmospheric sciences		•	•
Biochemistry	•	•	•
Bioengineering	•		
Biology	•	•	•
Biophysics	•	•	•
Chemical engineering	•	•	•
Chemical physics		•	•
Chemistry	•	•	•
Ecology and ethology	•		
Entomology	•	•	•
Genetics	•		•
Geology	•	•	•
Microbiology	•	•	•
Physical science	•		
Physics	•	•	•
Psychology	•	•	•
Plant Biology	•		
Teacher education in biology	•		
Teacher education in chemistry	•		
Teacher eduaction in earth science	•		
Teacher education in physics	•		
Veterinary medical science		•	•
Veterinary medicine (professional)	9	9	9
Zoology	•	•	•

• Foreign students should not consider applying to a health or medical related program.
7 This curriculum prepares researchers only.
8 This curriculum prepares students for positions as speech pathologists, audiologists or clinicians.
9 Foreign students are not accepted in veterinary medicine.

impression that you are a person who does not think, plan, or care about your work! So, remember, first read through the form from start to finish!

Universities want you to give the information they ask for in the spaces provided on the forms. Attach extra pages to your application only when absolutely necessary.

What we look for are

- complete records and transcripts
- meticulous attention to completing all blanks
- neat, clear printing
- a demonstration of understanding what has been asked

–Admissions Officer

Practice

EXERCISE 4-6

Look at the form. Read the instructions below before filling in the form.

Please print.

Name of applicant: _____
                        Last (Family)   First (Given)

Male ☐   Female ☐   Country of citizenship: _____   Birthdate: __/__/__
                                                                    Month Day Year

1. Fill in your name.
2. Fill in your address.
3. Fill in your date of birth.
4. Fill in your sex.
5. Fill in your marital status.
6. If your father or mother were born outside of the United States, don't fill in the form.

If you started filling in the form, you failed! This was a reading exercise! Before you start filling in a form, read all of the instructions very carefully!

EXERCISE 4-7

Look at the completed application form in Appendix 4, pages 144-146. Then answer the following questions.

1. Is the form for graduate or undergraduate applicants?
2. Is it a special form for international students?
3. How many sections are there?

4. Where do you sign the form?

5. Which section is "for office use only"?

6. Which section is optional?

7. Which section is about money?

8. Which sections are about tests?

9. Which question requires the longest answer?

EXERCISE 4-8

Look at sections of the application forms for universities A, B, C, and D in Figure 4B. Answer the questions about A, B, C, and D on the next page. If you cannot answer the question from the section of the form shown, answer with a question mark (?). The first one has been done as an example.

Figure 4B. Application Instructions

A

APPLICATION FOR ADMISSION

NEW STUDENTS ONLY
This application cannot be processed unless accompanied by a $10.00 application fee. This fee is non-refundable and is assessed one time only.

WASHTENAW COMMUNITY COLLEGE
4800 East Huron River Drive
P.O. Box D-1
Ann Arbor, Michigan 48106
(313) 973-3300

B

UNIVERSITY OF CALIFORNIA
INTERNATIONAL STUDENT UNDERGRADUATE
APPLICATION FOR ADMISSION 1992–1993
Nonrefundable Fee Required: **$40.00** for each campus.
Make check or money order payable to:
    THE REGENTS OF THE UNIVERSITY OF CALIFORNIA
Please type or print in black ink.

FOR UC USE ONLY					
(1) ☐ $40.00	(4) ☐ $160.00	(7) ☐ $280.00
(2) ☐ $80.00	(5) ☐ $200.00	(8) ☐ $320.00
(3) ☐ $120.00	(6) ☐ $240.00	(9) ☐ _____

C

INDIANA UNIVERSITY
International Application for Admission

Office of Admissions
Bloomington, Indiana 47405, U.S.A.

Please print or type.   Indiana University is an Equal Opportunity/Affirmative Action Institution.

This application is to be filled out by all non-United States citizens and those educated in countries other than the United States who wish to study in any division of Indiana University at any level—whether candidate for a degree or not. All information except the signature should be typed or printed plainly.

All graduate applications for August entrance must be complete, including all supporting documents, and in this office by March 15. Applications for January and June entrance must be in by October 15 and March 15 respectively. (Applicants to the undergraduate level will be considered six weeks beyond the dates indicated.)

Application fee: A nonrefundable application fee of $35 is required of every applicant. A check or money order should be enclosed when returning the application form.

D

International Student
Application for Graduate Studies

Office of Admissions
University of Houston
4800 Calhoun Road
Houston, Texas 77004
USA

**Note: This is a pressure sensitive form. Please print or type in the space provided.
DO NOT WRITE in the shaded areas, and return BOTH copies to the address above.**

	A	B	C	D
1. What is the application fee?	$10.00	$40.00	$35.00	?

2. Does this university require you to type your answers?
3. Will this university return your money if you're not accepted?
4. Will this university accept cash?
5. Does this section of the form give a mailing address?
6. Does this section of the form tell you where to attach the fee?
7. Does this university accept personal checks?
8. Is this application for undergraduates only?
9. Does this university require that the application be sent airmail?

Questions and Answers

I filled in three forms and they asked for my last name first. I've just filled in the fourth form, with my last name first, but now I see it says "First name, Middle name, Last name." What can I do?

You must correct it! But you may make your form look messy. So correct it carefully by erasing, by using correction fluid (a white liquid used to cover writing), or by covering the words with a small piece of white paper. If possible, make a copy of your form and the corrections may not look so bad.

Note: You can send in copies of the form, but your signature must be original—a copy of your signature is not acceptable. So when making copies of your completed forms, don't forget to put a piece of paper over where you have signed and then sign the new copy.

I started to fill in part of the form and then realized that it was "for office use"—in fact, it was shaded. Does it matter?

Yes, it does matter—since it shows that you didn't read the form before you began writing! The admissions office uses those parts of the form to collect statistics, to check details, and to make decisions. If possible, erase or cover your error and make a photocopy of the form. That way it won't look so messy. But see the above note about photocopying forms.

Courtesy of The University of Arizona

How Do I Complete the Application Form?

► **GIVING PERSONAL DATA**

► **APPLYING FOR A COURSE OF STUDY**

► **DEFINING YOUR RACE**

► **DESCRIBING YOUR ENGLISH LANGUAGE SKILLS**

► **WHAT I LEARNED IN SCHOOL**

► **DESCRIBING YOUR EMPLOYMENT EXPERIENCE**

GIVING PERSONAL DATA

What's your name? How do you spell it?

These are two very frequent questions that sometimes cause problems for international students. Why? Well, U.S. names tend to follow one fixed pattern, but some international students have different ways of giving their names in their countries or different ways of spelling their names.

What's most confusing for me? It's the names: How many? What order?
–Admissions Officer

Why is the way you give your name so important? Many universities are enormous institutions. For example, the University of Michigan has 36,000 students. The university keeps and uses records of all these students and of all the students who have ever attended the university. So you can imagine how important your name is—it is the first way to distinguish you from the other students.

Another way to distinguish students is with assigned identification numbers. Each U.S. student has a Social Security number (SS #). It has nine digits, e.g. 123-45-6789. A student's Social Security number is important because, in such a large group, there may be two or three or more students with the same name! When you arrive in the United States, the university will give you a student identity number to use in place of a Social Security number.

Another important distinguishing fact about you is your date of birth. Be sure to give it in the standard U.S. style of month/day/year.

Finally, there is your address. Of course, the university needs to know exactly where you are (your current mailing address) so that they can send you information—and an offer of admission! If you will be moving, or if you want your mail sent to an address different from where you live—make that clear!

Remember, you are only one of thousands of students! Therefore you must be

- Consistent. Give your name and other personal details such as age and address the same way every time
- Clear. Write very legibly
- Correct. Don't make any spelling or typing mistakes

Study the examples in Figure 5A. Iris has filled in her form consistently, clearly, and correctly, but Jung Hee hasn't. He has made seven mistakes.

Figure 5A. Two Sample Applications—One Correct, One Incorrect

A

SECTION A

Please indicate the semester you wish to begin studies at UH:

☑ Fall *1994*

☐ Spring

P I U A

Enter your social security number below: It will be used as your student identification number and assist us in our efforts to serve you. A temporary file number will be assigned by the Office of Admissions, if you do not have a Social Security number.

Name:

W O N G | I R I S | S U E M A Y
3 LAST (FAMILY) | 4 SUFFIX | 5 FIRST | MIDDLE

Name (if different from above on previous academic records):

W O N G | S U E M A Y
6 LAST (FAMILY) | FIRST | MIDDLE

Permanent Address: *LAI KING ESTATE*

F L 1 2 3 4 F O N G K U N G H O U S E ^ *HONG KONG*
7 NUMBER & STREET | COUNTRY

K O W L O O N | 3 8 1 8 2 4 5 6
8 CITY | 9 STATE | 10 ZIP CODE | 11 | 12 TELEPHONE

Present Address: *As above*

13 NUMBER & STREET | COUNTRY

14 CITY | 15 STATE | 16 ZIP CODE | 17 | 18 TELEPHONE

Telephone (daytime):

3 8 1 8 2 4 5 6
19

B

WESTERN MICHIGAN UNIVERSITY
APPLICATION FOR INTERNATIONAL STUDENTS
Application fee of U.S. $15.00 required (non-refundable)

Name of Applicant *Jung Hee Park* Social Security Number *922 12 41*
Family (Surname, Last) | Given (First)

PRESENT HOME ADDRESS *Seoul-City Young deungpa-Gu,*
Number | Street

Yeida da, Hangying-Apt 11-209 Korea
City | State/Province | Zip (Postal) Code | Country

PRESENT MAILING ADDRESS *As above*
Number | Street

City | State/Province | Zip (Postal) Code | Country

Sex_____ Male/Female Married/Single_____ M/S Citizenship *Korea*
Country

Date of Birth *3-5-68* Month, Day, Year Country of Birth *Pusan*

Practice

EXERCISE 5-1

Look again at Jung Hee's form in Figure 5A. Circle the 7 mistakes that he made. Now fill in the form in Figure 5B. Wait! Did you

- Read the instructions first?
- Fill it in in pencil?
- Have a friend check it?

Figure 5B.   A Blank Application Form with Instructions

Section I: Personal Information— All Applicants

1. **Legal Name:** Print your full legal name (last, first, middle, suffix) in the space provided. Leave at least one space between names. (Use this name on all your correspondence to the University.)
2. **Name on Academic Records:** If your name on any of your academic records is different from your legal name, print it in the space provided. If your legal name and the name on your academic records are the same, leave Item 2 blank.
3. **Social Security Number:** Print your social security number, and be sure to record it accurately. If you do not have a social security number, leave Item 3 blank. Please read the Social Security disclosure statement on page 2 of the application form before you complete this Item.
4. **Date of Birth:** Print your date of birth, including the month, day and year.

5. **Sex:** Check the appropriate box.
6. **Permanent Address:** Print your permanent address in the space provided. Include your street number and name, city, state, zip or other code, county (if in California), and country (if it is not the United States). If your address changes after you apply, send your new address to the processing service (see first page for address).
7. **U.S. Telephone Number:** If your permanent address is in the United States, print your area code and telephone number.
8. **Mailing Address:** If your mailing address is different from your permanent (home country) address, complete this Item; otherwise, leave it blank.
9. **U.S. Telephone Number:** Indicate the area code and telephone number at your mailing address if it is different from your permanent telephone number. Otherwise, leave it blank.

The Social Security number you provide on this form will be used by the University to verify your identity. Disclosure is mandatory. This notification is provided to you as required by the Federal Privacy Act of 1974. The University's record-keeping systems relating to this application were established prior to January 1, 1975, pursuant to the authority granted to The Regents of the University of California under Article IX, Section 9, of the California Constitution. If you are a United States citizen and do not have a Social Security number, apply for one through the nearest district Social Security Office and notify the Admissions Office when you receive it. If you are not a United States citizen and live in another country, it is not necessary for you to secure a Social Security number.

*OPTIONAL

Questions and Answers

I don't have a Social Security number. What do I do?

Read the instructions. Some forms tell you to leave the space blank, especially if it is a form where you will fill in boxes, like A in Figure 5A. For forms like B in Figure 5A, it is better to write "None."

Will I be penalized if I don't fill in all the blanks?

Read the instructions! In general, it is better to fill in all the blanks and write a separate cover letter explaining any special circumstances.

If an answer is "No" or "None," write that. For example:

Have you enrolled in this program before? ___*No*___

If it doesn't apply to you, write "N/A" (Not applicable), and explain if possible. For example:

You are applying as a Freshman ___*N/A*___ Transfer ___*N/A*___ *Non-degree student*

However, if a question is optional, you do not have to answer it. Typical optional questions are about race, marital status, and sometimes about age and handicaps.

On official documents I use both my father's and mother's name. Is my mother's name a "suffix"?

No. Suffix here generally refers to the custom of naming children with exactly the same name as a parent. In the United States, the typical suffixes are Junior (Jr.) and Senior (Sr.). For example, if a father and son have exactly the same name, Henry Jones, the father is known as Henry Jones, Sr., and the son as Henry Jones, Jr.

What does "MI" mean?

"MI" stands for middle initial. An initial is the first alphabet letter of a name. Andrea Sonia Wodzinki's middle initial is "S." Americans often use only the initial of their middle names, for example, John D. Brown or José R. Pérez.

APPLYING FOR A COURSE OF STUDY

On all forms there is a section that asks which course of study you want to follow. You usually give information on

- The term and year in which you want to begin
- The level at which you want to enter
- The degree you hope to receive
- The department in which you wish to enroll

Some examples from application forms are shown in Figure 5C. Undergraduates can write "undecided," which means that you can think about your major during the first two years. In the first two years all undergraduates take basic courses in the sciences, social sciences, arts, and humanities. U.S. students often spend these first two years finding out what they really like and what they are good at. If you have a clear idea of

Figure 5C. Courses of Study on the Application

A Mohammad Alsadeqi's Form

Select the college, curriculum, and major you wish to enter and write your selection in the space provided. See page 6 for the list of code numbers. Also refer to page 5 for special instructions which govern the election of certain majors.

Check College Desired —

Indicate Intended Major

☐ Business Administration ☐ Education ☐ Engineering

☐ Liberal Arts ☐ Lifelong Learning ☐ Mortuary Science

☐ Nursing ☐ Pharmacy and Allied Health Professions ☐ Social Work

_____
Curriculum Name

Enter the College, Curriculum and Major code numbers from page 6.   College_____ Curriculum _____ Major _____

COLLEGE/CURRICULUM/MAJOR

	Col	Cur	Major		Col	Cur	Major
Business Administration				**Law**			
* Accounting	F	G1		Pre-Law	A	12	
* Finance	F	G7		**Liberal Arts**			
* Management	F	G3		General/Undecided	A	07	000
* Marketing	F	G6		American Studies	A	01	046
Pre-Accounting	A	03	501	Anthropology	A	07	527
Pre-Combined General Business				Arabic	A	07	553
and Mortuary Science	A	03	502	Art	A	01	002
Pre-Marketing	A	03	503	Art History	A	01	005
Pre-Finance	A	03	504	Biology	A	01	037
Pre-Management	A	03	505	Chemistry	A	04	529

B Mi Soo Lee's Form

1. DEGREE SOUGHT/IF NONE, INDICATE SPECIAL STANDING (SEE APPLICATION COVER SHEET)	APPLICATION FOR ADMISSION	3. ADMISSION REQUESTED

APPLICATION FOR ADMISSION

THE GRADUATE COLLEGE
BOWLING GREEN
STATE UNIVERSITY

3. ADMISSION REQUESTED

YEAR   FALL   SPRING   SUMMER

19 _____ 1 ☐ 2 ☐ 3 ☐

2. DEPARTMENT OR INTERDEPARTMENTAL PROGRAM | MAJOR

4. SOCIAL SECURITY NO.

DEPARTMENTS AND INTERDEPARTMENTAL PROGRAMS	MAJORS	DEGREES OFFERED	DEPARTMENTS AND INTERDEPARTMENTAL PROGRAMS	MAJORS	DEGREES OFFERED
	Technical Writing	MA	Romance Languages		MA,MAT
Geography	Same	MA,MAT		French	
Geology	Same	MS		Spanish	
German	Same	MA,MAT	Sociology	Same	MA,MAT,PhD
Grad Bus Adm	Same	MBA	Special Education		MEd
Guidance & Counseling	Same	MA,MEd		Educ Ment Ret	
Health & Phys Ed		MEd		Train Ment Ret	
	Elem Phys Ed			Learn Dis &/or	
	Health Ed			Behavioral Disorders	
	Sec Phys Ed			School Psychology	
History	Same	MA,MAT,PhD	Theatre	Same	MA,PhD

MA — Master of Arts	MS — Master of Science	MOD — Master of Organizational Development	MFA — Master of Fine Arts
MAT — Master of Arts in Teaching	MAc — Master of Accountancy		EdS — Education Specialist
MEd — Master of Education	MBA — Master of Business Administration	MRC — Master of Rehabilitation Counseling	SpApplBio — Specialist in Appl. Bio.
MM — Master of Music	MHE — Master of Home Economics		PhD — Doctor of Philosophy

PLEASE TYPE OR PRINT   PLEASE REMOVE COVER SHEET BEFORE RETURNING APPLICATION TO THE OFFICE OF GRADUATE ADMISSIONS

what you want to specialize in, however, then you should fill in the name of your proposed major and make your interests clear in your "statement of purpose."

Graduates always know what they want to study! Because your field of study is often very specialized, this also means that it may be difficult to find a course that is the right level and content for you. For example, if you are not sure that polymer physics is the right course for you, write a note saying this and attach it to your application form. Also in your statement of purpose, state clearly what you have already studied and what you hope to achieve. This will help the admissions committee send your application to the right department.

Practice

EXERCISE 5-2

Look at the excerpts from the application forms and the lists of courses in Figure 5C. Use the following information to complete the forms.

1. Mohammad Alsadeqi wants to be an accountant. He has just finished secondary school and hasn't studied accounting before. Therefore, he must take a preaccounting course as an undergraduate.

2. Mi Soo Lee is a senior. She'll graduate with a B.A. next summer. She is applying to graduate school. She wants to major in business administration and begin in the fall of 1994.

Questions and Answers

Some application forms ask "Have you previously applied to ____?" Why?

If you have applied to the university before, your documentation will be on file, and this will save you and the admissions office a lot of time. You may want to update your scores, research or work record, or recommendations, but you will not have to fill out all the forms again.

It's February. I want to go to the university in September, but I don't know if I can take all the tests in time. What should I put on the form?

Universities use a semester or a quarter system. Most students begin their studies in the fall semester/quarter—in September or early October. Check your time schedule before you answer this section of the form; the processing fee applies to that semester only, and it is nonrefundable. This means that if you have delays and you are unable to arrive in time for that semester, you will have to reapply. You usually have to pay another processing fee.

DEFINING YOUR RACE

Some application forms have a section that asks for information on your ethnic group. This information is often marked "optional" or "voluntary," which means you don't have to fill it in. It may have a title such as "Demographic Information" or "Federal Aid Survey" or "Ethnicity."

What is ethnicity? If you look at the history of the United States, you see that immigrants came from many different countries in South America, the Pacific Islands, the Far East, India, Asia, Europe, and all over the world. For a time in the past, certain ethnic groups did not have an equal opportunity to go to school or the university. Since the Civil Rights Act of 1964, the federal government keeps statistics on the number from each ethnic group in universities, schools, and jobs. The purpose is to make sure that the imbalance is being changed and that there is now equal opportunity for all groups. Sometimes government funding is given to the university to be used as financial aid to encourage students from under-represented groups to attend.

Figure 5D.   Ethnicity Section

Please identify your ethnic background. Although this information is voluntary, it is requested to fulfill reporting obligations of the University. This information will remain confidential.

(1) ☐ American Indian or Alaskan Native   (2) ☐ Asian or Pacific Islander

(3) ☐ Black non-Hispanic   (4) ☐ Hispanic

(5) ☐ White non-Hispanic   (6) ☐ Other (please specify) _____

ETHNIC BACKGROUND DEFINITIONS:

American Indian or Alaskan Native — A person having origins in any of the original peoples of North America, and who maintains cultural identification through tribal affiliation or community recognition.

Asian or Pacific Islander — A person having origins in any of the original peoples of the Far East, Southeast Asia, the Indian Subcontinent, or the Pacific Islands. This area includes, for example, China, India, Japan, Korea, the Philippine Islands, and Samoa..

Black non-Hispanic — A person having origins in any of the black racial groups of Africa.

Hispanic — A person of Mexican, Puerto Rican, Cuban, Central or South American or Spanish culture or origin, regardless of race.

White non-Hispanic — A person having origins in any part of the original peoples of Europe, North America, or the Middle East.

Other — None of the above.

Most forms say that this information is confidential and is not used in application decisions, but your "cooperation will be appreciated." Figure 5D is an example of an "ethnicity" section.

Practice

EXERCISE 5-3

These words often appear in sections on ethnicity. Match each word with its best definition.

1. gender   a. working together
2. handicap   b. do something without being forced
3. disability   c. open to choice
4. cooperation   d. male/female
5. voluntary   e. a disadvantage that affects success
6. optional   f. inability to do something

Questions and Answers

Will I be penalized if I don't fill in the section on ethnicity?

No. In fact, this information is collected only for U.S. citizens and permanent residents. The university does, however, keep statistics on international students with regard to (1) citizenship (what passport you hold), (2) visa (what kind of visa you have), (3) location (where you come from), and (4) race (what ethnic group you belong to). Summary statistics about this information are published in books about international education in the United States.

DESCRIBING YOUR ENGLISH LANGUAGE SKILLS

All universities are concerned about your level of English. They expect you to join the regular classes with U.S. students and understand the lectures, read the textbooks and journals, write—usually type—the assignments, and do well in the exams.

Almost all universities require you to take an English proficiency test such as the TOEFL before admission. And many have their own English exam, which often includes an oral interview. Some students may feel resentful that they have to take another English test when they arrive. After all, they have been accepted by the university, and they arrive exhausted from a long journey.

The reason for the English test is that most universities have found that students need more skills to succeed in their academic work than the TOEFL measures.

I have applied for financial aid at several universities and each promised to finance me because of my excellent academic work. My problem was in the English test. I couldn't get financial aid until I passed the Michigan test.—*Student*

Students with insufficient ability in English may take longer to complete their studies. They may have to take lighter loads, drop courses, be placed on probation. Therefore, the purpose of the placement exam is to make sure that students get special help with their English, if they need it.

When filling out the form, it is important to be honest about your proficiency in English. For example, answer this question: Do you find it difficult to understand the sections of the application forms in Figure 5E on the next page?

Figure 5E. Language Proficiency Section

A

5. List below the languages which you know, and indicate for each language your degree of proficiency in reading, writing, and speaking:

Languages	Degree of proficiency (native, good, fair, or poor)		
	Reading	Writing	Speaking
ENGLISH			

6. Which of the above is your first (home/native) language? _____

B

LANGUAGE PROFICIENCY

Proof of proficiency in the English language is required before you may begin your academic study. What is your current competency in the English language?

☐ Native Speaker   ☐ Excellent   ☐ Good   ☐ Fair   ☐ Poor   ☐ No previous study

If your answer is no, then maybe you are not being completely honest. Many U.S. students ask for help with these application forms!

Practice

EXERCISE 5-4

The following words are often used to describe a student's command of English. State whether each descriptive word is positive or negative.

1. excellent
2. native
3. fluent
4. very good
5. fair

6. weak
7. poor
8. proficient
9. competent
10. good

EXERCISE 5-5

Complete the excerpt from an undergraduate application form.

> Write a paragraph describing your English language education (number of years, number of hours per week, teaching methods used, language skills emphasized).

Questions and Answers

I would like to go to the United States, study English there, and then apply to a university. Is this a good plan?

Many students do this. There are good intensive English programs in the United States to prepare you for the TOEFL and for academic work.

I can understand my English teacher and the English in our textbook, but when a visitor from the United States spoke to our English class, I couldn't understand one word. Usually I get 95 percent on my tests, but now I am worried.

Often it is easy to understand English in a textbook but not everyday, spoken English. It takes time to become accustomed to different accents, dialects, speed, and vocabulary—U.S. students and professors use slang that you won't find in a textbook. Many students get a shock when they arrive and find they can't understand anything. But after a few weeks, it's a lot easier!

My English tutor will help me fill in the form and will check my essay so that I won't have any mistakes. Is this okay?

Yes and no! It is good to have someone else read through your form and check for mistakes. The personal statement part of the form, however, you must write yourself.

WHAT I LEARNED IN SCHOOL

"How was school?" "What did you learn in school today?" Maybe your parents asked you these questions when you got home from school. Now you have to describe this experience—and in positive terms! If you did well at school, you must be able to prove it. If you did poorly, you must be able to explain it.

Every country has a different system of education. In the United States, terms such as *GPA, credit hours, school profile,* and *class rank* are familiar to U.S. students. These terms often appear on application forms. You may have to fit your own educational experience into these categories.

We want to know what kind of academic work they have done—specifically and satisfactorily completed.–*Admissions Officer*

Admission officials need to know if you are a serious student and if your education up to now qualifies you for admission. Read the admissions information carefully. It will tell you whether you are qualified to apply. When admission officials look at your application they will consider

* Your educational level—how much education you have had
* Your educational achievement—how well you did
* What kinds of schools you attended—their general quality
* Your suitability for their university and program—how academically well prepared you are

Admissions officers know that your educational system may be different from the U.S. system. They do not want to accept you if you do not have the educational background to do well at their university. They want to accept you if you do.

In general, on the application form it is best to write the name of your school, examination results or grades, and school leaving certificate or degree awarded using the terms used in your country. For example, a student from Germany applying for undergraduate study might list on his form that he has the *arbitur (zeugnis allgemeiner hochschulreife)*. A student from the Soviet Union might have the *matura/attstat*. A student from Turkey might list the *devlet lise diplomasi*. Admissions officers who admit international students are usually quite familiar with the names of exams and degrees from various countries.

If you think admissions officers will be confused by your educational background, you can explain the situation in a separate letter. Any information (names, certificates awarded) that you provide in your letter should be consistent with the information that you list on the application form.

Be as precise as possible about your academic background. Some students may have attended secondary schools in which the curriculum is more advanced than in most U.S. high schools. Students from such academic backgrounds may be admitted to begin undergraduate university work at the sophomore rather than freshman level. In other cases, students may have attended undergraduate university programs that are not as extensive as some U.S. universities. These applicants might not be admitted for graduate studies but might be admitted for high-level undergraduate studies.

In addition to listing information about your educational background on the application form, you must provide documents from the schools you attended to prove that what you list on your application form is true. When such documents are not written in English, you are expected to provide an official translation of the documents. (You will learn about this in Chapter 8.)

Sometimes they list all their secondary education, and you have to determine what is college-level work and what isn't.–*Admissions Officer*

All application forms ask for

- The name of your school
- The location of the school
- The dates you attended
- Your examination results or degrees

Some applications ask you to begin with your primary or elementary school; others with your last school or university. If your school or university changed its name since you attended, be sure to include the old and new name when you list that school.

Often the space on the form is very small. If it is absolutely necessary, you may continue on a separate page.

Practice

EXERCISE 5-6

Review your educational life. Begin with your primary school. On the left side of a large piece of paper, write the first year you went to school and continue up to the present year. On the right side of the page, write down all the information you can remember about each year of your education. Then use the facts that can be documented to complete your application forms.

It's difficult to explain the meaning of the national college entrance exam. The system of grading is different.–*Student*

EXERCISE 5-7

Study the model in Figure 5F on the next page. Then, in pencil, fill in the blank form with your information. Practice writing in tiny, neat, clear letters!

Another problem—listing abbreviations for university names or places of previous work.–*Admissions Officer*

Write the names and addresses of your schools, employers, examinations, and awards in full. Do *not* use abbreviations, shortened forms of written words.

DESCRIBING YOUR EMPLOYMENT EXPERIENCE

Most, but not all, application forms have a section for employment. U.S. high school students often have part-time jobs. For example, they work after school or in the summer—in stores, restaurants, or offices—for a few hours a week. As undergraduates, they may take a part-time job at the university (a work-study position) or a job off campus.

International admissions officers know that this may not be common in other countries. However, they want to get an understanding of the "whole you"—your experience, responsibilities, skills, interests, finances, etc. Moreover, for graduate applicants especially, if your job experience is related to your field of study, it will help your application.

Part of understanding the kind of person you are is reading your "life story"—what you have done every year of your life. This is why application forms ask you about school, jobs, and military service; and some say "Please account for all the time since high school." Others may ask for jobs in the past year, or only full-time jobs. If you leave a gap—an unexplained few months or years—they will want to know why. So if you were in the hospital, or prison, or the army, or just on vacation, explain this!

Always provide information about educational, work-related or other experiences in logical order. Do not jump around in time. Most ap-

Figure 5F.   Academic Information

A

ACADEMIC INFORMATION

| 17 Name of high school (secondary school) Osaka International School | 18 City, state, zip Osaka   605 | 19 County Japan |

20 High school graduation date month **4** year **92**

21 American College Test (ACT) and Scholastic Aptitude Test (SAT)—see page 2 of form.   was taken ☑ACT ☐SAT   will be taken ☐ACT ☐SAT

22 ACT month **10** year **91**

23 SAT month ___ year ___

24 **IMPORTANT** Have you attended any post-high school educational programs? ☐ **Yes** ☐ **No**   If yes, list below. (Include all universities, colleges, schools of nursing, technical schools, BGSU course work or other programs.) If you plan to take any course work before attending BGSU, indicate this. Request that each school send an official transcript to the BGSU Office of Admissions. If you decide to take collegiate course work after you have submitted this application, you must inform the Office of Admissions. Failure to indicate college attendance may result in refusal of admission, no transfer of credit and/or expulsion from the University if discovered subsequently.

College or University (most recent first) (continued on back)	Location	from month	from year	to month	to year	credit hours attempted
Washtenaw Community College	Ann Arbor, Michigan	6	92	present		27

25a Are you currently under suspension or dismissal for academic or disciplinary reasons from any college, university, or post-high school education program?   ☐ yes ☑ no   If yes, attach a statement of explanation.

25b Has either of your parents earned a four-year college degree? father ☑ yes ☐ no   mother ☐ yes ☑ no

B

PART B. INFORMATION ABOUT THE APPLICANT'S EDUCATIONAL BACKGROUND

1. List below, in chronological order, with dates, every school you have attended, beginning with the time you entered primary school to the present, including each primary, secondary, and post-secondary institution. If you need additional space, please attach a separate page.

Name of institution attended	Location of institution	Dates of entering and leaving	Certificates, degrees, or diplomas. (not translated)	Date received

2. If you are now a candidate for any title, degree, or diploma, name the title, degree, or diploma and the date it is expected to be conferred _____

3. Previous (or current) university major(s): Undergraduate _____ Graduate _____

4. You should arrange for Indiana University to receive official or certified copies of your academic records throughout your attendance at secondary school, college, university, and professional institutions of learning. An exception is that those with the bachelor's degree or its equivalent need not send their secondary school records. Records should list the subjects studied and the grade, mark, or other evidence that each individual subject was completed to the satisfaction of the authorities in charge. Records should also include certified copies of any diplomas, degrees, or other certificates received. All records should be in English. If the language of the records is not English, a certified literal translation should be included with the original document. Since certificates and records filed for examination are not ordinarily returned, you should send certified/official attested photocopies if the documents in question cannot be easily replaced. Uncertified photocopies alone are not acceptable.

plication forms require you to give information in reverse chronological or chronological order. In most cases, the university wants you to begin with your most recent experiences and move backward in time.

Some universities don't ask for information on employment, but if it is relevant you can include it in your statement of purpose. The admissions officers want to know whether you

- Are a serious student
- Will do well in your studies
- Will need any special help
- Will add something valuable to the college

For graduate students, any research or teaching position is especially relevant. Some universities may want to know whether you have a position awaiting you when you finish your studies. All this information helps the admissions officers build up a picture of you as a potential "academic"!

Figure 5G gives some examples of the employment information requested.

Figure 5G. Employment Section

A

EMPLOYMENT — If you are currently employed, please indicate:

Employer: *Tokyo Insurance Company*
Job Title: *Personal Assistant*   Department: *International Operations*

B

PART D. INFORMATION ABOUT OTHER EXPERIENCE
1. Employment (List present or last employment first.)

Title of position	Name and address of employer	Type of work	Dates of entering and leaving
Personal Assistant	Tokyo Insurance Company 2-13-1 Minamisawa Higashikuruka City Tokyo Japan 203	secretarial and administrative	March 1990 to present

C

Employment and Practical Experience: Please list in reverse chronological order; attach additional sheet if necessary.

Name of Employer	Address and Telephone No.	Type of Work	Dates of Employment

Do you plan to be employed while at school?_____ If yes, how many hours per week?_____

Practice

EXERCISE 5-8

When she was filling out the employment section, Junko asked herself the following seven questions for each job she has had. The language from the form is on the left. Her answers are on the right. Read both carefully. Then ask yourself the same seven questions for each job you have had. Use your notes to fill out employment sections of application forms.

Where am I working now?	**What was my last job?**
1. reverse chronological order, present/last employer first	This means I begin with my current job. Well, my job now is as assistant to the manager. In my previous job I was a clerk.
	What is my job title?
2. job title title of position title	I'm a personal assistant. In my last job I was a clerk/trainee.
	What do I do?
3. nature of work type of work responsibilities	In my current job I write letters and reports, schedule meetings and take minutes at them, keep records, prepare the budget—mainly secretarial and administrative duties. In my former job I answered the phone, typed letters, and filed documents—mainly clerical and secretarial duties.
	Who do I work for?
4. employer company place of employment	Now I'm working for the Tokyo Insurance Company. Before I worked for the National Motor Corporation.
	Which office do I work in?
5. department	Now I work in international operations. In my previous job I worked in the general office.
	Where can they contact my employer?
6. address	Tokyo Insurance Company 2-13-1 Minamisawa Higashikuruka City	National Motor Corp. 1-2-3 Chuou-cho Meguro-ku
city	Tokyo	Tokyo
country	Japan 203	Japan 152
phone	03-3123-9810	03-3123-1234
	When did I work there?
7. beginning–end	I began working at TIC in March 1990, and I am working there now.
entering–leaving	I worked at NMC from March 1988 to March 1990.

EXERCISE 5-9

Look at the information Junko has given in Exercise 5-8. Complete the blank form in Figure 5G by filling in the details of Junko's work experience.

Questions and Answers

I started a job but I didn't like it and I left after three months. I felt bad about it. Do I have to put it on my form?

If the instructions say to account for all the time, you must mention it. Students often change their jobs. You won't be penalized.

I went from secondary school to the university. I've never had a job. Will this affect my application?

No. But think hard about your out-of-school experience. Have you worked as a volunteer (unpaid)? Describe any experience that shows your maturity, skills, interests, perseverance, and other positive qualities.

CHAPTER SIX

What Writing Do I Need to Do?

► **UNDERSTANDING WHAT TO WRITE IN THE PERSONAL STATEMENT**

► **WRITING THE PERSONAL STATEMENT**

► **REVISING THE PERSONAL STATEMENT**

► **WRITING A STATEMENT OF PURPOSE**

UNDERSTANDING WHAT TO WRITE IN THE PERSONAL STATEMENT

A personal statement is an essay that an individual writes about himself or herself. Some universities ask undergraduate applicants to write this in order to get an idea of the kind of person they are—their strengths and weaknesses. Students say it is difficult to write the personal statement. It *is* difficult, and it requires a lot of thinking, discussing, planning, writing, and revising—all of which take a lot of time!

Why do some universities ask you to write a personal statement? In your file the admissions officers have

- The application form with *facts* about your age, schools, academic records such as grades, English ability, etc.
- The letters of recommendation with your *teachers' opinions* about the kind of student you are, in and out of class
- The personal statement with *your opinion* about the kind of person you are

Now let's look at Maria. It's not a particularly aggressive essay, rather simplistic. Lots of C's and a low verbal score. But she's the best student in French and very social. The question is, should we push for her when she's not good academically?–*Discussion from an Admissions Committee*

They look at all these factors when they discuss which students to select. This is what happens. First, they reject students who fail to meet the requirements: for example, their grades are low, their English is weak, their finances are insufficient. Then a committee of faculty and admissions officers discusses the remaining applicants one by one. They want to choose students who together will make a good freshman class. In this class they want *variety*. For example, they look for

- Some very good students, some average, some below average (although in this case "average" means "very good"!)
- Some students with interests in the arts, some with interests in the sciences
- Some with special talents, for example, music, drama, sports
- Some from different backgrounds, for example, urban and rural, east and west coast, rich and poor, U.S. and international. The fact that you are an international student can be an advantage. Universities like to have students from wide geographical areas.

The "mix" of the freshman class is very important. For example, if you happen to be a brilliant chemist and a prize-winning chess player, you have a good chance of getting in, but if five other wonderful chess-playing chemists also apply, your chances become much smaller!

The reality is that you have no control over this situation, over the other students who apply, but you *can* control the impression you give in your personal statement by

- Being yourself
- Being honest
- Being clear
- Doing your best
- Not being modest

and, last but not least, by

- Expressing all of the above in a neat, well-organized, interesting essay.

Good, well-thought-out essays. Tidiness. Brevity.–*Admissions Officer*

Some students do their best but don't understand this situation and feel very disappointed when they are rejected.

Why should you care about extracurricular activities? Some universities make a very big deal of it and reject students who do well in school but don't have a strong talent of any kind.–*Student*

Some examples of ways universities ask for a personal statement are given in Figure 6A on the next page.

Practice

EXERCISE 6-1

It is very important to read the instructions for the personal statement carefully. Try it! Read the three examples in Figure 6A. Tell which ones specifically tell you to do each of the following. Answer *A, B,* or *C,* or *None.*

1. Handwrite the essay
2. Use black ink
3. Limit the length
4. Use an additional page if you want
5. Write your name on each page
6. Write about your career objectives
7. Answer a list of questions
8. Give reasons for studying in the United States
9. List your prizes and awards
10. Describe your work experience
11. Choose whether to write the essay or not

Figure 6A.   The Personal Statement Section

A

19. In your own handwriting and in English write an autobiographical statement which tells something of your life, special interests, your reasons for desiring to study in the United States and your plans after completing your education.

B

4. List, roughly in order of their importance to you, those activities and awards which you believe best represent your greatest achievements and interests. Tell us approximately how many hours per week each activity entails. Should you care to comment further, you may do so on additional sheets.

You may want to consider drawing upon the following areas in compiling your individual list of activities:

• Activities and organizations to which you have been a frequent contributor. [Include the year(s) of participation and any offices held.]

• Athletic teams on which you have played. (*Circle* year of participation if you won a varsity letter.)

• Community activities in which you have been involved such as scouting, volunteer work, religious youth groups, cultural organizations, or tutorial programs.

• Creative work, hobbies, or special training to which you have devoted substantial time and which you have pursued to the point of reasonable mastery.

• Prizes, honors, or special recognition you have won (scholastic, athletic, literary, musical, artistic or other).

• Travel or other experiences that have been especially rewarding.

6. In reading your application we want to get to know you as well as we can. We ask that you use this opportunity to tell us something more about yourself that would help us toward a sense of who you are and how you think. Your statement should be done *in your own handwriting*, and you may attach additional sheets if necessary.

C

Essays

The essay section provides an opportunity to describe your abilities in ways that grades and test scores cannot. It shows us your ability to organize thoughts and express yourself in writing. Please **respond to two** of the following three items. **Please write your essays on separate sheets of paper.**

1. What experiences led you to the selection of your professional objectives?

2. In addition to the information form, what other factors would you like the Board of Admissions to consider in evaluating your candidacy? Feel free to include some of your important accomplishments, your goals, or your ideas about education.
3. Describe a significant historical event in your country.

Questions and Answers

My handwriting is terrible. Why can't I type my personal statement?

If the instructions say to handwrite, then you must handwrite. If not, then you can choose. In fact, at the university level most professors require students to type their papers. Typed papers are much easier to read. However, many people believe that everyone should be able to write legibly and, moreover, that handwriting reflects character.

My form says "Write 200–250 words." Does it matter if I write more?

If the instructions give limits, you should keep to those limits. There is a reason for them. Maybe they want you to be precise, maybe they don't have time to read more. Ten or twenty words more might not make a difference, but two hundred more might irritate a busy admissions officer.

The instructions in the personal statement section say "Use this space to indicate briefly any additional information that would help us in considering your application for admission." There are ten lines. Can I write more?

The space limitation is not to restrict what you say but to encourage you to get to the point quickly! Write only key ideas, clearly and simply. If you do have special circumstances that will require more space to explain, write about these on a separate page and add a note to the section on the application form that says, for example, "Please see attached sheet for details."

What if I sound proud?

Just give the facts! The admissions officers need to know if everyone in your senior class gets an award for "excellent academic work" or if you are the only one of two hundred.

WRITING THE PERSONAL STATEMENT

Writing a good personal statement takes time and effort. Begin early and keep working at it until you're satisfied. But remember, there is no one "right" answer to the personal statement instructions; there is only the "write" answer! The instructions about the possible topics (your hobbies, activities, goals) are deliberately vague. This is so that there will be many different essays from students. (Can you imagine reading the *same* essay thousands of times?) And the best way to make your essay better is to write a lot and revise a lot. Tim Chin of the University of Michigan advises students, "Remember WORDS": W—Write it down; O—Organize; R—Revise; D—Discuss; S—Style.

The personal statement shows how well you can express your ideas in writing. Most of the time at the university your writing skill is very important to your academic success. Your grades will depend on your term papers, final exams, etc., and these are often in essay form.

As for the ideas you put in your personal statement, the instructions say "This is an opportunity for you to describe yourself in a way that the facts and figures on the application form can't." Make yourself come alive as a person.

Think hard about what you like doing, what you're good at, what you hope to achieve in life. For almost everyone, probably the hardest thing when writing an essay is getting started. Below are several activities to help you take the first step, writing it down.

At the end you will find your ideas are clearer. For example, Lani began writing of her worries about studying in the United States. She would be so far from her family. As she repeated the exercise, her ideas turned to the choice of major, to the possibilities of jobs back home after graduation, and the way education was valued in her society.

Practice

EXERCISE 6-2

1. Put a clock or watch in front of you.
2. Take a clean pad of paper.
3. Give yourself 10 minutes.
4. Begin free writing—start writing and don't stop! If you can't think of how to start, just write your name. Just keep your pencil moving and write down any ideas that come into your head. Don't worry about spelling, grammar, or vocabulary. If you don't know a word in English, explain it, or write it in your own language.
5. At the end of 10 minutes, stop.
6. Read through what you have written and underline anything you like.
7. Choose one of the ideas underlined as the starting point for a repetition of the exercise. Write it on a new page.
8. Repeat steps 1–7 as many times as you can.

EXERCISE 6-3

1. Read the instructions for writing a personal statement in Figure 6A, section B.
2. Begin brainstorming. That is, without hesitating, make a list of all the things related to the instruction that are important to you. Don't reject anything, even if it sounds crazy!
3. Go through the list. Can you put the ideas into groups?
4. Examine the "crazy" ideas. What can you learn from them?
5. Do a free writing exercise using the ideas from your brainstorming.

EXERCISE 6-4

1. Take a large sheet of paper—the bigger, the better!
2. Write your name in the middle and draw a circle around it.
3. Relax, open your mind, and think about your character, experiences, and other aspects of your life. For each idea about yourself that comes to mind, draw a line from your name and write the words, events, and feelings you had.
4. Use the ideas for a free writing exercise like the one you did in Exercise 6-3.

Questions and Answers

What if I have average grades and no special interests?

Talk to your parents, friends, and teachers. Talk about all the things you have done over the last few years. Compare yourself now with yourself of five days ago, or five months ago, or five years ago. Maybe things don't seem important to you but have impressed others. Look for patterns in your activities. For example, if you are a student who always helped out with the organization of activities, maybe your skills can be defined as those of a manager.

Who will read my essay?

The admissions officers will read your essay, and the committee. It will help them get an idea of you as a person. Your essay will go in your file. It won't be used for placement. However, the quality of your English will be examined, and you may be advised to enroll for special language classes if necessary.

REVISING THE PERSONAL STATEMENT

Now that you have a lot of ideas from your free writing and brainstorming activities, it's time to discuss it with your friends, teachers, and if possible a U.S. friend. Have you included all the relevant points, and only relevant points? Remember, you have a specific audience. You want the U.S. admissions officers to understand and enjoy your essay. You also have a specific purpose. You want them to select you for their freshman class.

These are seven steps to success

1. Limit your topic.
2. Set priorities.
3. Explain unusual circumstances.
4. Write a first draft.
5. Get a second opinion.
6. Revise, rewrite, revise.
7. Get it checked.

If you are applying to departments that offer vocational or professional programs, you may have to write a specialized essay. Your essay should show how your background has prepared you for the course of study. Look at the special instructions in Figure 6B, section B for applicants to natural resources, nursing, physical education, and music.

You want your personal statement to show how you are special, and not typical. Admissions officers say a typical, or "predictable" essay from a U.S. student is

- How I learned discipline and courage from sports
- How I traveled to Europe and broadened my experience
- How I felt terrible when my parents divorced

Figure 6B.   More Personal Statement Sections

A

X. ESSAY — ALL APPLICANTS

The essay is an important part of your application and may be a deciding factor for some campuses in accepting your application. This is especially true if you have selected a very popular field of study. Write your essay on no more than two sheets of 8½″ × 11″ white paper. Write on one side only. Type or use black ink and be sure to write your name at the top of each page. **PLEASE READ THE INSTRUCTIONS.** They tell you what to include in your essay.

B

 PERSONAL
STATEMENT

(23.) Write a brief personal statement according to the specific instructions below. **Limit the essay to one sheet and enclose with this application.**

Freshmen (Note exceptions listed below as specialized essays):

Provide a brief essay about your activities, interests, achievements, and talents. The goal of the essay is to help us get to know you as an individual. Point out your strengths and explain any inconsistencies in your record. You might comment on your experiences at school, in the community, or at work. Other possible topics are your educational and career objectives.

Specialized essays for applications to the following units:
School of Natural Resources, School of Nursing, or *Division of Physical Education:* Please provide *additional* comments to the above essay explaining your previous experience and interest in issues related to your educational and career goals.

Bachelor of Musical Arts in the School of Music: Include in your statement a description of your non-musical interests.

Transfer Students (Note exceptions listed below as specialized essays):

Provide a statement of educational purpose. If you know the field you wish to pursue, include your rationale for choosing that field. If there have been any interruptions in your education, explain the circumstances. Do you feel that this interruption has been advantageous or disadvantageous to your educational goals? If you have had any academic difficulties (poor grades, incompletes, drops, or term withdrawals), please explain.

Specialized essays for applications to the following units:
Architecture Program in the College of Architecture and Urban Planning: Essay may extend to 3 or 4 pages. Focus your essay on your background, interests and experience in architecture and related fields; comment on your career goals.

College of Pharmacy: See Supplementary Application.

C

Please attach a one-page statement in English in your own handwriting, commenting on your background, your educational objectives at Denison, and your career goals.

What would be a "predictable" essay from students in your country? How will you make your personal statement different?

You want your essay to be different from those of U.S. students, and from all the other students applying from your country. Think about what only *you* notice, only *you* have experienced. For example, if you travel, describe the particular things that you noticed other than the tourist sights. If you had a bad experience, describe how you overcame it. If you have developed skills and responsibilities in certain community activities (clubs, drama, music, sports, volunteer work, etc.), describe them and explain what you have learned from them.

- Make notes of your unusual experiences.
- Talk to your teacher or someone who can help you clarify your ideas.

An interesting extracurricular activity can polish an otherwise dull academic record.–*Admissions Officer*

The presentation of your work is as important as the contents. You should make a checklist like the one below and honestly answer each item *Yes* or *No*.

1. My ideas are clear. Three different people have read and understood everything.
2. My ideas are interesting. My three reviewers said it didn't put them to sleep—quite the opposite, they couldn't put it down!
3. My grammar and spelling are all correct. I have reviewed every word.
4. My essay is neatly written or typed. There are no messy corrections. I have used the same pen throughout. It is easy to read.
5. My name is on each page, so it won't get lost.

Questions and Answers

What if my English is weak?

Do your best. Review your grammar, punctuation, and spelling. Ask your teacher or a friend to check your first draft, not only for the English but for whether your ideas are clear. Getting this kind of help is okay, but having someone write the essay for you is not.

We are not looking for "long words"—these can make an essay sound foolish, "wordy." My advice is KISS—Keep It Super Simple!–*Admissions Officer*

WRITING A STATEMENT OF PURPOSE

Graduate students also report that it is very difficult to write the essay requested of them, which is usually called the statement of purpose, but sometimes personal statement. Read the section on the personal statement. Although the examples refer mainly to undergraduates, the principles are the same for graduates. The difference for graduates is that most universities

- Ask for a statement of purpose
- Want it to be very specific about academic experience
- Consider it an important factor in selection

In your statement of purpose, you should make a strong case for yourself. If you have unusual experience, explain it. Don't leave it to be interpreted in the wrong way. If you have weak scores, address this question, and turn it to your advantage if possible. If you have something to say, say it! Be clear and to the point. Don't be too modest.

You should tailor your statement of purpose to the specific university program. When you are sending more than one, you may be able to keep the key ideas the same, but you must alter details for different programs:

- Highlight the interests of the faculty—refer to your interests in their research areas, but avoid mentioning a member of the faculty by name.
- Ensure that a number of the faculty share the same interests as you and that the faculty contains more than one person with whom you would like to work. Remember, professors move and you don't want to arrive there only to find your favorite professor is on sabbatical!

Practice

EXERCISE 6-5

The selection committee will probably ask the following questions about all the applicants. Can you answer these, directly or indirectly, with regard to *your* skills and experience?

1. Has José done research? Does he know what will be expected of him?
2. Has he made a presentation at a professional meeting? Has he published? submitted articles?
3. Can he communicate? Research also requires skills in writing and presenting his work in English to be disseminated.

Questions and Answers

I have had a number of interesting short-term jobs during my school vacations. Should I mention these in my essay?

Some application forms say "you may omit summer and part-time work." However, if your job was relevant to your field of study, then you will want to be sure to mention it in your essay.

I telephoned the admissions office to check on the status of my file and was told to call back after the lunch hour. I felt I had wasted my time and money. Is it okay to telephone if I have a problem?

Yes. However, when you telephone you must remember that admissions offices are busy and handle hundreds of applications. Have all your questions ready. Write them down before you actually make the call.

The person who answers the telephone may not have the information you need, and the person who has the information may not be available. If this happens be sure to ask for the name of the person you will need to speak to and ask when (date and time) you should try to call. It may be possible for you to leave a message for the person. If you leave a message, explain who you are and why you are calling. Be as brief as possible.

When you telephone, remember the time difference between where you are and where the university is located. Most administrative offices are open from 9 A.M. to 4:30 P.M., but are closed between 12 M. and 1 P.M. for lunch. It is probably best to telephone between 10 and 11 A.M. or 1:30 and 3:00 P.M.

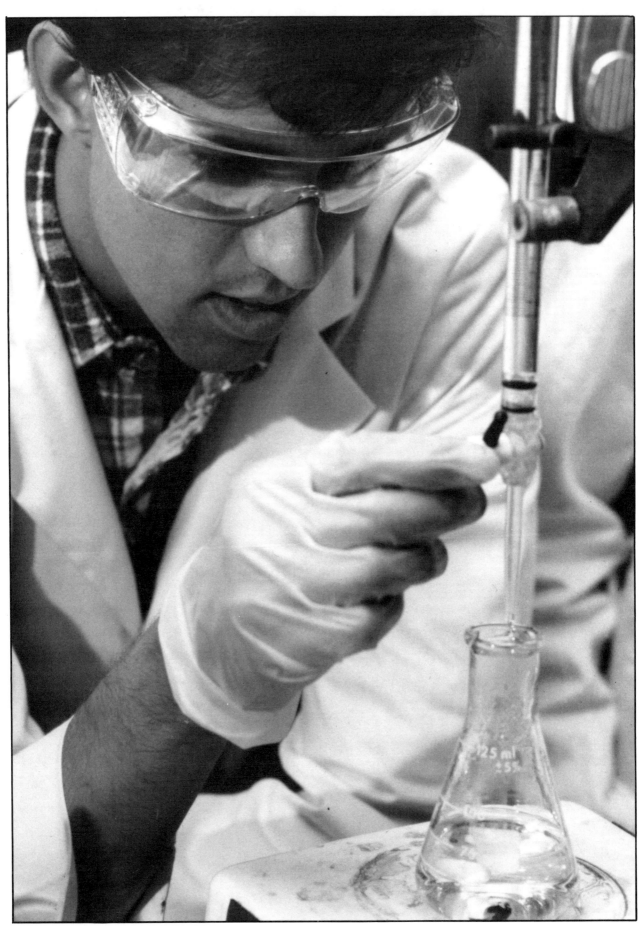

CHAPTER SEVEN

How Do I Pay for My Studies?

► **WHAT FINANCIAL ASSISTANCE IS AVAILABLE?**

► **FINANCIAL ASSISTANCE FROM THE UNIVERSITY FOR GRADUATE STUDENTS**

► **PROVIDING FINANCIAL CERTIFICATION**

WHAT FINANCIAL ASSISTANCE IS AVAILABLE?

University education in the United States is not free. Students must pay to attend class, to buy books, for a place to live, for food, and for other items. These costs can also vary substantially depending on 1) your personal situation, for example, whether you are a single undergraduate or a graduate student with a family, and 2) the university and the specific program within a university that you will be enrolled in.

Advisors to international students report that the biggest problems these students have are financial problems. The costs of studying and living in the United States continue to increase from year to year. Students must plan for these increases in costs.

Many international students are studying in the United States with financial assistance, but students *must* establish the support *before* coming to the United States.

Financial assistance may come from

- The international student's own government
- Private companies
- International organizations
- The U.S. universities themselves

International education center libraries have books that list financial assistance funds available to international students. A new reference book published by the Institute of International Education is *Funding for U.S. Study: A Guide for Foreign Nationals.* Write to

IIE Books
809 United Nations Plaza
New York, NY 10017
USA

When a student applies for financial assistance from an educational organization or private company they have to fill in the organization's application form, which often asks for the same information university applications ask for. Usually such awards are for students who are studying a specific subject area of interest to the organization. For example, an ecology student might get a grant from the World Wildlife Fund for a special biological habitat study.

Students need to be neat and complete when applying for grants. You wouldn't believe some of the messy, scribbled applications I've seen from students who are asking for thousands of dollars of financial assistance.–*USIS Educational Advisor*

Generally, international students are *not* eligible for the federal (U.S. government) financial assistance that is available to U.S. residents. At public, state-supported universities and many other colleges and universities, most of the financial aid for U.S. undergraduates is from federal financial aid programs. If an applicant is eligible for federal financial aid, the university will tell the applicant what special form to use and how to get the form. To be eligible for U.S. federal aid does *not* mean, however, that a person is definitely going to receive aid. A U.S. citizen or eligible noncitizen (such as a permanent resident or temporary refugee) must apply for federal aid.

Some universities have some scholarship funds available to especially well-qualified international undergraduate applicants. Often such funds will pay for tuition costs but not for living costs. Small, private colleges and universities may have more funds available to assist international students, but a small college may accept only a few international students.

At the graduate level, if nonfederal funds are available to assist students with expenses, international students are also eligible for such assistance. Often financial assistance awards to graduate students are made by the department in which a student will study.

State universities will ask you if you are a resident of that state, and how long you have lived there. If you are a U.S. citizen or eligible noncitizen and have lived in a state for over a year, making this state your "domicile"—your home, the place where you live—you will be eligible for the in-state tuition fee, which means you pay a lower tuition fee. For example, a U.S. citizen or eligible noncitizen who is a resident of Iowa will pay the in-state tuition fee at a state university in Iowa; however, a student who is a permanent resident of Illinois attending the same university in Iowa will have to pay the nonresident fee, which is higher. International students coming from overseas are also charged nonresident fees at state universities.

A very helpful booklet, entitled "Financial Planning for Study in the United States," is published by the College Entrance Examinations Board, New York, New York 10023, USA, and is available at USIS centers and other international educational centers. The table of contents is shown in Figure 7A on the next page.

Practice

EXERCISE 7-1

Scan the table of contents in Figure 7A to answer the following questions.

1. On which pages in this booklet might you look for information on the different costs to consider?

2. Assistance from universities does not usually include money to travel from the student's home country to the United States. On which page might there be information on how to get such money?

3. How many kinds of housing seem to be described in this booklet?

4. IIE (Institute of International Education) is an agency that administers many educational exchange programs. The office in New York provides information about study opportunities but does not accept applications directly from students. Where might you find the postal address for IIE in this booklet?

5. On page 36 there is information about loans. What are loans?

6. Where in this booklet would you find advice from international students?

Figure 7A. Contents of "Financial Planning for Study in the United States"

A

Financial Planning for Study in the United States

A Guide for Students from Other Countries

B

Contents

Foreword   3
Introduction   6
Costs of studying in the United States   8
▪ Application expenses   8
▪ Travel   8
   Travel insurance   9
   Travel grants   9
▪ Tuition and fees   10
▪ Housing and food   11
   University housing   11
      Dormitories   11
      Cooperatives   12
      Graduate living units   12
      Living groups   12
      Married student housing   12
   Nonuniversity housing   12
      Furnished rooms   13
      Apartments   13
      Food   13
      International Houses   13
   Payments   14
▪ Books and supplies   14
▪ Medical and dental services   15
▪ Health insurance   15
▪ Clothing   16
▪ Incidental expenses   17
   Vacation expenses   17
   Summer expenses   18
▪ Expenses for married students and
      their dependents   19
      Housing   19
      Food   19
      Health expenses and insurance   19
      Schools   20
      Child care   20
▪ Extra expenses for graduate students . . .   20
▪ Typical expenses for an academic year   21
▪ Orientation and English-language programs . .   22
Types of financial aid available
      to foreign students   23
   Sources of financial aid outside the
      United States   24
   Governments   24
   Organizations   24
   Educational credit agencies   24

▪ Awards from
      United States government sources   27
▪ Aid from organizations   28
   Institute of International Education   28
   Agencies serving
      particular nationality groups   29
      African-American Institute   29
      American-Mideast Educational and
         Training Services. Inc.. (AMIDEAST) . . .   30
      International Human Assistance Program .   30
      American-Scandinavian Foundation   30
      Latin American Scholarship Program
         of American Universities   31
      North American Association of Venezuela .   32
▪ Aid from United States colleges
      and universities   32
   Undergraduate aid   32
   Graduate aid   33
      Scholarships   33
      Fellowships   33
      Assistantships   33
How to apply for financial aid
      from United States institutions   35
Financial resources after arrival
      in the United States   36
▪ Loans   36
▪ Employment   36
   Summer employment   38
Seeking help in case of financial emergency .   39
Final arrangements regarding finances   40
▪ The obligation of a private sponsor   40
▪ Problems of currency restrictions and
      transfer of funds to the United States . . .   40
▪ Using United States banking services   41
▪ Money needed during the first few weeks
      in the United States   42
▪ Protecting personal funds en route
      to the United States   42
Advice from foreign students now in
      the United States   43
Sample budget form for the first year   44

Reprinted from the 1984 edition of *Financial Planning for Study in the United States: A Guide for Students from Other Countries* by permission of the College Entrance Examination Board, New York, New York 10023, U.S.A.

Figure 7B.   U.S. Department of Education Student Aid — General Information

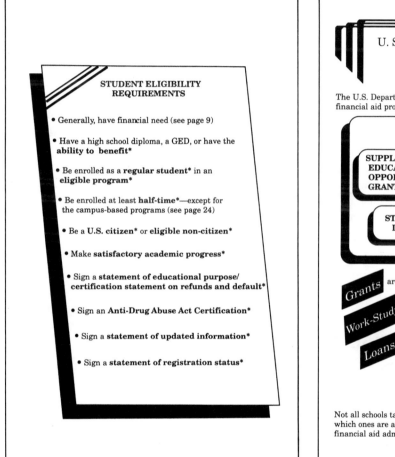

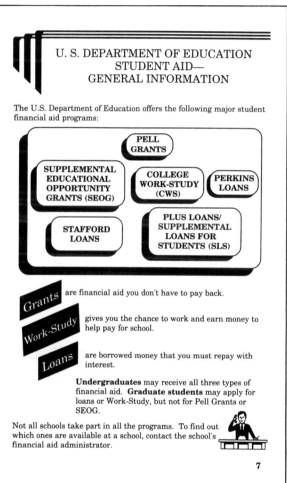

Used with permission of: U.S. Department of Education.

EXERCISE 7-2

Read the following profiles about the background of student applicants. Then read the eligibility requirements in Figure 7B. Which students may be eligible for federal (U.S. government) financial aid?

1. Javier was born in Venezuela. He came to the United States with his family when he was seven years old. He attended elementary school, junior high school, and graduated from high school in Miami, Florida. He used to be a citizen of Venezuela, but he is now a U.S. citizen.

2. Geraldo was born in Italy. He came to the United States when he was eleven years old to live with his uncle when his parents died. He attended junior high

school and high school in New York City. He is a permanent resident of the United States, but he is still an Italian citizen.

3. Desta was born in Ethiopia. He attended elementary school and secondary school and completed two years at a technical university, all in Ethiopia. When he was in Europe for a football game, he applied for refugee status at a U.S. embassy and eventually was given refugee status and was sent to Ohio to live. He now wants to continue his university studies in the United States.

Questions and Answers

I received information about a private organization in Washington, D.C. that says it will help me get financial aid through private organizations and businesses. If I send them information about me and pay them a $60 fee, they will send me a list of organizations that will give me assistance. It says I am guaranteed to get a scholarship. Should I send them my money?

No, probably not. You may be cheated. Talk to an educational advisor before using such an organization. Even if you do get a scholarship, it may only be for a small amount—for example, $100, which will not cover much of your educational expenses.

Also, be careful about organizations that *guarantee* to find you a place at a U.S. university. You may lose your money. Unless you have a government sponsor in your country, it is your responsibility to apply to U.S. universities and to stay informed.

FINANCIAL ASSISTANCE FROM THE UNIVERSITY FOR GRADUATE STUDENTS

The "small print" of the instructions sent by the university tells students how to apply for different kinds of financial aid. Many graduate students hope to get a part-time job as a teaching or research assistant (TA/RA). Working for the university as a TA or RA means

- You have a small salary
- You may not have to pay tuition

The job is described in terms of the percentage of a full-time job that you work, e.g., a .25 or a .50 appointment. TAs may assist in an undergraduate course, lecturing, working in a lab, grading papers, and helping students with individual problems during office hours.

If you want to apply for an assistantship position, generally you should emphasize any research or teaching experience you have had. Your application documents should provide evidence of your special skills or qualifications. There may be many qualified applicants competing for only two or three financial awards. It is the applicant's responsibility to show how he or she is special and well-suited for an award.

Other sources of income are fellowships. All students can apply for these. They can also request tuition waivers.

Practice

EXERCISE 7-3

Read the excerpts below. Respond to the following statements by writing *True* or *False.*

1. I can apply for only one graduate appointment.

2. I may have to send documents and test scores.

3. A fellowship is the same as an assistantship.

4. If I work half-time I don't have to pay tuition.

5. All students can apply for fellowships.

A

16. If recommended for admission:

    a. I wish to receive consideration for financial aid at the University of Illinois. ☐ Yes ☐ No

       If "Yes," type of financial aid desired (indicate first, second, and third choices by numerals 1, 2, and 3):

       ☐ Assistantship   ☐ Fellowship   ☐ Tuition waiver only

       For: ☐ One term ☐ Academic year ☐ Academic year and summer session

       Beginning (month only)_____, 19_____

       Number of dependents (optional information)_____

    b. I must receive financial aid from the University of Illinois to enroll. ☐ Yes ☐ No

B

7. Applicants who are seeking financial assistance through graduate appointments should mark "Yes" and complete item 16 on the application form. An applicant can apply for more than one kind of appointment by designating the order of preference. Additional supporting documents and test scores, if required by your major department, must be sent directly to the department using the address found on the enclosed Departmental Code and Address Listing. Students who are not applying for admission or readmission must use a separate application for graduate appointment to apply for assistantships, fellowships, and tuition waivers. The form is available from the Graduate College, University of Illinois at Urbana-Champaign, 122 Coble Hall, 801 South Wright Street, Champaign, IL 61820, U.S.A.

Three kinds of appointments for graduate students are available at the University of Illinois at Urbana-Champaign: fellowships, assistantships, and tuition waivers.

    a. *Fellowships.* Students in all departments are eligible to apply for fellowships. Fellowship stipends vary with the type of award. Federal, state, industrial, endowed, and institutional fellowships, which sometimes carry higher stipends, are also available and are described in the University of Illinois *Graduate Programs* catalog. Most fellowships, including University Fellowships, provide for waiver of or exemption from tuition. Fellows in many fellowship programs may accept an assistantship of up to one-fourth time. The salary received for the assistantship is in addition to the fellowship stipend and is in most cases taxable.

    b. *Assistantships.* Teaching, research, and laboratory assistantships carry minimum salaries of about $4,630 (as of 1987-88) for one-half time for the academic year. Assistants are exempt from tuition, if the appointment is for at least one-fourth time and not more than two-thirds time, and if the assistant serves for at least three-quarters of a term.

    c. *Tuition Waivers.* These awards provide exemption from tuition. They are restricted to students who will be registered for at least 3 units of work.

For University Fellowships, assistantships, and tuition waivers, there are no restrictions as to citizenship, age, sex, ethnic or national origin, or marital status. Certain federal, industrial, and special fellowships have stipends and restrictions differing from those for University Fellowships. Candidates for such awards should consult with the appropriate departmental officer.

February 15 is the deadline for receipt of all papers pertaining to applications for most fellowships and tuition waivers. Some departments have established earlier deadlines (for example, the School of Music deadline is February 1, with the additional deadline of January 15 for applications in the area of voice). These deadlines do not apply to applications for assistantships; certain industrial, endowed, and special fellowships; or tuition waivers. However, most graduate appointments are assigned by April 1.

Fellowship awards will be announced about March 15. The University adheres to the resolution adopted by the Council of Graduate Schools in the U.S. Under the terms of this resolution, the recipient of an award who accepts it before April 15 may resign before or on that date in order to accept another appointment. After April 15, however, another award may not be accepted without obtaining formal release from the first commitment. It is understood that the award of a graduate appointment for one year involves no commitment for continued support by the University for subsequent years.

Since fellowship and assistantship decisions are made by April 1 for the following fall semester, a student who requires assistance in the form of a fellowship, assistantship, or tuition waiver to finance his or her first year of graduate study at the University should not plan to attend if an offer has not been made by early May.

EXERCISE 7-4

Read about Kim's situation below. Refer to excerpt B in Exercise 7-3 to complete each statement with the correct dates.

Kim has applied to the music department to get a Ph.D. He has looked at the costs of studying and living at the university. He knows he needs a TA position for .50 time, or a fellowship and a TA job for .25 time. He has good grades, speaks English well, and has tutored students at home and in his school. He has filled in the forms and sent his documents, the details of his scores, and a cover letter to the department. Now he is examining the schedule to see when he should hear news of his appointment.

1. He must send in his application to the music school by

    February 1   February 15   March 15   April 1   April 15   early May

2. He must send in his application for the fellowship by

    February 1   February 15   March 15   April 1   April 15   early May

3. He will hear about the fellowship by

    February 1   February 15   March 15   April 1   April 15   early May

4. He must accept or reject the fellowship by

    February 1   February 15   March 15   April 1   April 15   early May

5. He will hear about the graduate appointment by

    February 1   February 15   March 15   April 1   April 15   early May

6. It's unlikely he'll be successful if he hasn't heard by

    February 1   February 15   March 15   April 1   April 15   early May

PROVIDING FINANCIAL CERTIFICATION

Financial certification is a guarantee that a student has enough money to pay for the course of study in the United States. *All* universities require some kind of form or document that shows financial ability. The certificate is signed by the person who agrees to be responsible for the expenses.

The certification form may be called

- A statement of financial responsibility
- A confidential statement on finances
- A confidential statement for financing studies
- A declaration of finances
- A financial resources certification

Other financial documents that some universities ask for are

- A letter from the guarantor (the person who agrees to be responsible for the expenses)
- A bank statement
- A copy of an award letter from a sponsoring agency
- A copy of an award letter from a university department

Figure 7C. Forms and Information on Financial Ability

A

The Ohio State University

Official Financial Statement for International Students

You must complete this form as completely as you can and return it to the Admissions Office. Your admission may be delayed if this statement is not returned.

Please read the following before completing both sides of this form:

The Ohio State University requires that you complete this form to indicate what your sources of funding will be for the length of your study at Ohio State. No applicant will be admitted without proof of adequate funds, because the Immigration and Naturalization Service (INS) regulations require the University to verify that any applicant admitted will have sufficient funds to meet all educational and living expenses while attending. For a summary of current educational costs and living expenses at Ohio State, consult "Estimated Expenses" in the application instructions.

The Ohio State University will issue either an I-20 or IAP-66 in order to enable you to obtain a student visa after you have: (1) received a positive academic decision, (2) provided evidence of English proficiency, and (3) shown evidence of adequate financial resources through the completion of this form. Admitted students sponsored by a government, agency or organization will be issued a Form IAP-66 for a J-1 visa which may have a two-year home-country residency requirement. Other students will be issued a Form I-20 for an F-1 visa.

If admitted, you will need to prove to the United Sta
retain copies of all financial documents submitted in

Undergraduate Applicants Note: The Ohio State U
international students. Because of this, we do not end
while pursuing a degree at Ohio State.

Instructions for Completing this Form

All applicants should complete Section A, "Person
supported by personal and/or family funds, complete
agency, or organizational scholarship, have your spo
but are applying for a graduate associateship, indica

Section A. Personal and Family Inform

Name (as it appears in your admission application):

Tong
Family Name

Are you currently in the U.S. with a non-immigrant v

If yes, indicate visa type (for example, F1, F2, e

If J-1, who issued the IAP-66: _____

Do you plan to bring any member of your family wit

If yes, please provide the following information i
if more space is needed):

Name

_____
_____
_____
_____

B

Section B. Affidavit of Support for Persons Sponsored by Personal/Family Funds

Applicants supported entirely by governmental, agency, or organizational scholarship should leave this section blank and complete Section C.

I, _Tong, Chang_ _father_ , do hereby promise to provide
  Name of Sponsor   Relationship to Applicant

educational and living expenses for _Fung-ha Tong_ as
     Name of Applicant

indicated below (check one or more of the following sections if they apply):

☐ I will provide full support for the applicant, for his/her entire period of study at The Ohio State University. I certify that I have sufficient funds to cover the minimum cost of the first year of study as indicated in "Estimated Expenses" in the enclosed application instructions.

☐ If the applicant brings his/her spouse and/or children, I will provide full financial support for them for the duration of the student's education at The Ohio State University.

☐ I will provide partial support for the applicant's period of study as indicated below (complete the following):

I will provide $ _12,000_ per year (Indicate in U.S. dollars)

beginning _9/1/93_ and ending _6/1/95_ .
   month/day/year   month/day/year

As verification of the section(s) checked above, I am providing the applicant with a Certified Bank Statement in English, indicating the current balance on deposit and current exchange rate for one U.S. dollar and additional documentation, if necessary, showing availability of funds for first year of study.

Signature of Sponsor _Tong Chang_ Date _12/15/92_

Section C. Affidavit of Support to Be Completed by the Government, Agency, or Organization Sponsoring the Applicant

This section must be completed by your sponsor, even if the sponsor is submitting a separate statement of your award. Such a statement must be on official letterhead and include all of the information requested below.

Please Print

We, _____ , hereby certify that we will pay the following
     Name of Sponsor

expenses for Mr./Miss/Mrs. _____

_____ tuition, fees, and OSU health insu
(OSU health insurance required)

Study is approved for _____

Columbus, Ohio. The scholarship is effe

ESTIMATED EXPENSES FOR 1989-90

The figures indicated below represent the minimum level of estimated expenses for 1989-90. You should plan for an increase in tuition and living expenses of as much as 5% to 10% per year.

Tuition and Fees

For Students Enrolled In:	Non-Resident Tuition Per Quarter	Books & Supplies for Academic Year (9 months)	Total of Tuition and Books Academic Year (9 months)	Total of Tuition and Books Full Year (12 months)
Undergraduate Colleges	$2,093	$ 390	$ 6,669	$ 8,892
Graduate School	$2,590	$ 390	$ 8,160	$10,880

Health Insurance

International students are required to purchase health insurance throughout the duration of their study. In addition, we recommend that they purchase insurance for family members who accompany them.

	Quarterly Premium	Total for 12 months
Student	$ 89	$ 356
Student and Spouse	$216	$ 864
Student and Children	$279	$1,116
Student, Spouse and Children	$408	$1,632

Living Expenses

The following are minimum estimates of student and family living expenses and include housing, utilities, food, clothing, local transportation, laundry and miscellaneous personal expenses. Costs for books and insurance are itemized above and not included here. Your expenses will vary depending upon the type of housing you choose and your personal life style.

	Expenses for 12 months
Single Student	$ 7,624
Student and Spouse	$10,984
Student, Spouse and One Child	$12,622

(for additional family members, add $136.50 per month for children up to 12 years of age and $280 per month for older children and adults)

In addition to completing the *Official Financial Statement* form, you must provide proof that you have funds to cover all expenses your first year of study for yourself and any family members who accompany you to the U.S. for a specific time period. See "Financial Requirements" for details about what to submit.

As an example, to compute the amount needed for one year, use the above tables and add together (1) total of tuition and books for 9 or 12 months, (2) insurance for 12 months for you, and (3) living expenses for 12 months. For example, a single graduate student's expenses for the one year would include $10,880 for tuition and books (4 quarters), $356 for insurance, and $7,624 for living expenses for a total of $18,860.

The amounts given above are the minimum students need to meet the most basic expenses while attending Ohio State and living in Columbus. However, we recommend that students bring additional funds, if possible, to insure that they will be able to meet living expenses without difficulty. Additional funds are helpful in meeting living expenses comfortably, and in covering educational expenses such as research costs, academic-related equipment and supplies, thesis and dissertation costs, and field trips.

If you have a family member or a sponsor who is able to provide additional money for your studies, but you need authorization from Ohio State to arrange for release of the funds, contact the Office of International Students and Scholars (OISS) upon your arrival at Ohio State.

C

What You Must Submit

What financial documents you are required to submit depends on who is supporting you.

• *If you are fully self-supported*, you must submit the Official Financial Statement and a bank statement indicating you have the full amount needed for the first year. You must also submit a statement describing how you will support yourself for the duration of your studies.

• *If you are supported by a family member or a friend*, that person must complete and submit the enclosed Official Financial Statement indicating that funds are available for the full length of your educational program. Your financial sponsor must also provide a bank statement, or other documentation indicating that sufficient funds are available for the first year of study.

• *If you are supported by an organization (agency, institution, or the government)*, your sponsoring organization must complete and submit the enclosed Official Financial Statement in order to verify that you will receive support. If the amount they award does not meet the minimum required (see the box for "Estimated Expenses for 1990-91"), you will be asked to provide proof of additional funds to cover the balance.

• *If y
uat
gra
the
the
"Estimated Expenses for 1990-91"),
you will be asked to provide proof of additional funds to cover the balance.

• *If your funding is from more than one source*, each source should provide proof of the amount and length of time the funds are available.

Graduate applicants may be eligible for financial support in the form of graduate associateships or fellowships. See the section "Financial Information" for more details. If you intend to apply for associateships or fellowships, please indicate your intention on the *Official Financial Statement* form.

Advanced Deposit of Funding

Applicants who will be relying on funds from Ghana, Guyana, Iran, Lebanon, Liberia and Nigeria will be required to make an advanced deposit for the full cost of their first year of study. Ohio State requires an advanced deposit if an applicant's funds are coming from any country that has severely restricted or prohibited the transfer of currency to students in the U.S. Countries other than those indicated above may be added to the list if it becomes clear that students cannot transfer currency from them.

D

The U.S. admissions officer needs a financial document that states

- The amount of financial support available per calendar year
- When the guarantee begins and ends
- The applicant's full name
- The guarantor's name and address
- The guarantor's relationship to the applicant or official job title of the signer if the guarantor is an organization

The certificate should have an original signature, an official seal, and the name of the university. If the guarantor is a sponsor, the certificate should include

- The degree and major of the applicant
- A list of expenses covered by the sponsor

A university must know that a student's funds are guaranteed for at least the first year. Some universities require documents that show that the funds are available for the whole program of study—four years for a bachelor's program, two years for a master's program, etc.

If it is not in English, the financial certificate should be accompanied by an official translation. Figure 7C shows some of the forms and instructions connected with financial ability.

Practice

EXERCISE 7-5

Choose the word that gives the best meaning for the underlined word or phrase.

1. You may, *in lieu of* a financial form, send a certified bank letter addressed to the university.

    a. in addition   b. before   c. in place of

2. The Board of Regents *reserves the right to* change tuition and fees at any time.

    a. has authority to   b. will never   c. expects soon to

3. You are required to *submit evidence of* sufficient funds for living expenses during the summer months, regardless of whether you intend to enroll as a student during the summer term.

    a. show certification   b. borrow money for   c. pay a deposit for

4. The information you provide shall remain *confidential*.

    a. public   b. private   c. available

5. All estimated expenses for nonimmigrant international students are based on *nonresident* fees.

    a. not a permanent resident of the state

    b. a foreign-educated student

    c. a student not living on campus

EXERCISE 7-6

Look again at the financial statement for a student applying to Ohio State University in Figure 7C. Then answer the questions.

1. Is Fung-ha Tong being supported by a government agency or by his family?
2. How much support per year is shown?
3. Is the support sufficient to meet expenses at Ohio State?
4. Fung-ha Tong is applying for a graduate program in mathematics. Where else might he be asking for assistance from?
5. What else does Fung-ha Tong need to send with this form?

EXERCISE 7-7

Compare the two financial certificates in Figure 7D, one for a student from Jordan and one for a student from Taiwan. Look at the list on page 108. Which is a more complete certificate? What information is missing from the certificates?

Figure 7D.   Two Examples of Financial Certificates

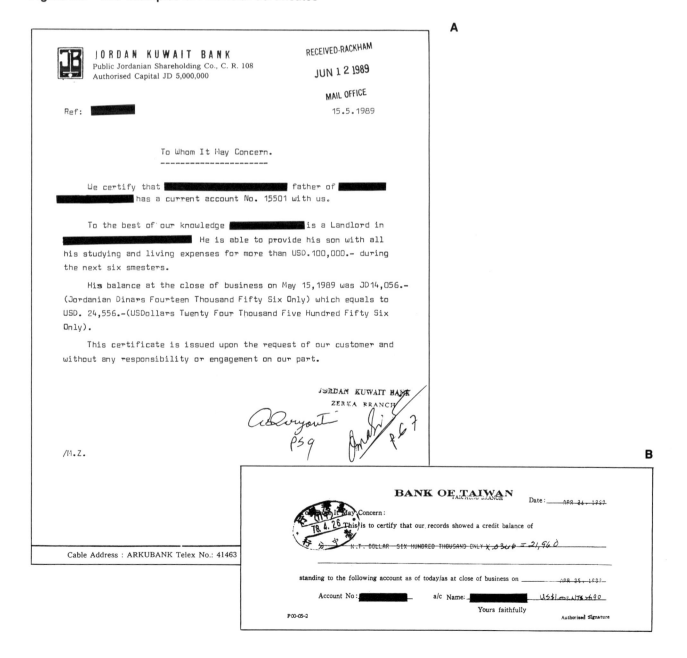

Figure 7E.   A Completed Confidential Statement of Finances

Financial
Certification

17. Confidential Statement of Finances

Source of Funds	Yearly Amounts (in U.S. dollars)				Total Amount for All Years
	1st	2nd	3rd	4th	
Personal Savings*	$ _____	$ _____	$ _____	$ _____	$ _____
Parental Support*	$ _____	$ _____	$ _____	$ _____	$ _____
Scholarship (indicate name of sponsor)* Royal Thai Government	$ _____ $ 20,000	$ _____ $ 22,000	$ _____ $ 25,000	$ _____ $ 28,000	$ _____ $ 95,000
Other Sources* _____ _____	$ _____ $ _____	$ _____ $ _____	$ _____ $ _____	$ _____ $ _____	$ _____ $ _____
Yearly Totals	$20,000	$22,000	$ 25,000	$ 28,000	$ 95,000 Grand Total

*All personal and parental funds listed above must be documented by bank statements; funding from scholarships and other sources must be documented by official letters stating the amounts of funding available and for what period of time. *PLEASE NOTE:* Xerox or other electrostatic copies are *NOT* acceptable.

EXERCISE 7-8

Use the information in Figure 7E to answer the questions.

1. How is this student being supported?
2. What is the total amount being guaranteed by the sponsor?
3. Why do the yearly amounts increase?
4. Will there be a problem if this student's application does not include a letter from the sponsor?

EXERCISE 7-9

How will you pay for your university education?

Pretend that you must show that you have enough money for three years of U.S. study—$15,000 for the first year, $16,500 for the second year, $18,000 for the third year. (The costs go up because of inflation. Universities increase their fees accordingly. Rents usually increase each year, too.) Do you have sufficient funds? If not, you should be looking for sources of financial funding from your own country.

Questions and Answers

Why are students from some countries asked to make a deposit of the funds for the first year of study?

It is very difficult to transfer money out of some countries. Universities have found that some students arrive in the United States for study but can not get their money out of their country to pay for their tuition and living expenses.

I'm applying for financial assistance. I do not have any funds available to certify.

At some universities, you may be recommended for admission on the basis of your academic record and English ability. You may be granted some kind of financial assistance, but the award will not cover everything. The university will then notify you with the amount of funding that you must certify you have available to support you. The certificate of eligibility for a visa will not be awarded until you provide financial certification.

Why should I keep a copy of my financial certification?

You will need it when you go to the embassy to apply for a visa.

What will happen if the university expenses are more than the amount of the financial certificate?

If university funds are available for assistance, the student, if academically well qualified, may receive some assistance from the university. If no university funds are available, the applicant must be rejected. A certificate of eligibility for a visa cannot be offered if a student cannot document enough funds.

Courtesy of Larry Murphy/University of Texas at Austin

What Else Must Be Completed to Apply?

► **BUILDING A COMPLETE APPLICATION**

► **GIVING PROOF OF YOUR EDUCATIONAL BACKGROUND**

► **ARRANGING FOR REFERENCES/LETTERS OF RECOMMENDATION**

► **UNDERSTANDING THE VISA PROCESS**

► **FINISHING UP**

BUILDING A COMPLETE APPLICATION

Each university has specific requirements about what an applicant must send them. You must read carefully the application information from each university.

Undergraduate and graduate information will be different. The graduate information from various departments may list special application requirements.

In the information, there may be a list to help you remember what you need to do. Admissions officers know that the procedure is complicated and confusing, so they provide a *checklist*.

An example is shown in Figure 8A. Use the checklist. It can help you stay organized.

Practice

EXERCISE 8-1

Read the checklist in Figure 8A and complete these statements.

1. The application form and all the documents should be sent
    A. Separately—each document in a different envelope
    B. In one envelope
    C. In two envelopes

2. An application fee
    A. Will be sent to the applicant
    B. Must be sent by the applicant with the application
    C. Can be sent after the applicant is admitted

3. According to the checklist if you are applying as a freshman to this university, how many other things in addition to the application form must be sent to the university?
    A. Three   B. Eight   C. Ten

4. An applicant who has been attending another university in the United States does not need to send
    A. The application fee
    B. Secondary school reports
    C. SAT scores

5. After an applicant sends the documents (such as school academic records), the university
    A. Returns them if the student is not admitted
    B. Returns them after the student is admitted
    C. Keeps them whether or not the student is admitted

6. A freshman applicant at this university needs a TOEFL score
    A. Not less than 550
    B. If English is his or her native language
    C. If he or she has not taken the SAT

Figure 8A. A Sample Application Checklist

Checklist for Application Completion

Use the following checklist of procedures as a guide in preparing your application. Please try to submit all the required documents at one time in one envelope. If you cannot send all requested items at once, please indicate when you expect to send them.

I have enclosed with Application	I will send by ___ (give date below)	**To enter Boston University as a Freshman, you must send:**
_____	_____	1. The completed application form, pages i–iv, found in the center of this booklet.
_____	_____	2. The thirty-five dollar ($35) application fee. Payment must be made by check in U.S. dollars, payable to Boston University, and marked clearly with your full name. Please do not send currency.
_____	_____	3. Official Scholastic Aptitude Test (SAT) results. The SAT is required of all freshman applicants. Arrange to take the SAT at least six months before the date you wish to enter.
_____	_____	4. Official Test of English as a Foreign Language (TOEFL) results. You must take the TOEFL if English is not your native language. **A score of 550 on the TOEFL is expected.**
_____	_____	5. Official transcripts or records of your last four years of secondary school, with a certified English translation, if necessary.
_____	_____	6. Certified copies of results of any qualifying or national examinations you have taken, with a certified English translation, if necessary.
_____	_____	7. Your completed Confidential Statement for Financing Studies at Boston University. If you cannot obtain certification directly on this form, attach a certified bank letter or credit reference from your sponsor's bank.
_____	_____	8. The two required essays described on page iii of the application.
_____	_____	9. A letter of recommendation from one of your teachers or counselors. If the letter is not written in English, it must be accompanied by a certified English translation.
_____	_____	10. An essay detailing what you have been doing since you left your last school, if you are not currently attending a secondary or post-secondary school.

		To enter Boston University as a Transfer, you must send:
_____	_____	1. All documents requested for Freshmen listed above. However, the transfer applicant, who has completed, at the time of application, one full year of study at the university level, will not have to submit the results of the SAT.
_____	_____	2. An official record or transcript from each post-secondary school you have attended. Your records should indicate the number of lecture and/or laboratory hours per week and the grade you received for each course.
_____	_____	3. An official catalogue or syllabus from each post-secondary school you have attended, in English, if possible, containing course descriptions and degree requirements.

Mailing Instructions
Applicants should forward in one envelope (using a mailing label from this booklet) the completed application, the fee, and all supporting materials. If you are unable to enclose some documents with the application, indicate on this form when you plan to send the missing documents, and enclose this form with your application.

Note: All documents you submit become the property of Boston University.

Undergraduate Programs Bulletin
The *Boston University Undergraduate Programs Bulletin* contains detailed information about the academic programs offered for undergraduates at Boston University. The information includes descriptions of the University's undergraduate Schools and Colleges, degree requirements, faculty, and courses.

If you would like to receive a copy of the *Undergraduate Programs Bulletin,* please fill out and return the Bulletin Request Form inserted in this booklet. If you want the *Bulletin* sent to an address outside of the U.S., please include a check or international money order for the amount of five U.S. dollars ($5) made payable to Boston University to cover mailing costs.

7. A freshman applicant who has already finished secondary school also must send

    A. A larger application fee

    B. Another essay explaining what he or she has been doing

    C. A catalog from his or her secondary school

8. An applicant who has completed the form and has most of the documents ready but is waiting for a letter of recommendation from a teacher should

    A. Wait until everything is ready and then send everything

    B. Send what is completed and include the checklist with a note saying when the recommendation will be sent

    C. Send in what is completed and hope that the admissions officers do not notice what is missing

Questions and Answers

The instructions say I should send in my test scores. I thought the test organization sent the scores directly to the university.

Yes, official results are sent to the university by the test organization. However, you must remember to list all the universities you want to receive your scores when you take the test. You can send a photocopy of your test results with your application to show you have taken the test, but the university must receive results directly from the test organization.

Why do universities want me to send everything together?

It can be very confusing to receive documents separately. At a large university, hundreds of pieces of mail arrive every day. Your document might not end up in your file. *Note:* When you send documents always make sure that your name is on the document—the same name as on your application form!

Admissions officers cannot make a decision on your application if any of your documents are missing. If your documents arrive past the deadline, they will not be able to admit you. If any financial aid is available for international students, you will miss that, too.

I am not asking for financial aid. My family will pay all my educational expenses. Why do I need to send a financial statement?

To be admitted to a university and to be sent a certificate of eligibility for a visa, you *must* provide official statements to the university to prove you have the funds to pay for your studies.

A university, by U.S. immigration law, should not admit a student unless the applicant can show

- Academic ability
- English language ability
- Financial resources sufficient for the program of study

GIVING PROOF OF YOUR EDUCATIONAL BACKGROUND

Undergraduate applicants need to provide academic records for all the secondary schools they have listed on the application forms. Graduate applicants must provide academic records for each college, university, or post-secondary school attended. The records should show grades, marks, rank in class, and examination results.

Official academic records of courses taken are called *transcripts*. If your transcript is in your native language, you need to provide an official translation.

Figure 8B shows three examples of academic certificates. Figure 8C is a transcript.

Figure 8B.   Three Sample Academic Certificates

A

BANGKAPI GOVERNMENT SECONDARY SCHOOL

BANGKOK 10240, THAILAND

To whom it may concern :

This is to certify that ▮▮▮▮▮▮▮▮▮▮▮ of Bangkapi Government Secondary School, born on August 23, 1954, passed the Final Examination of the Upper Secondary Education held by the Ministry of Education, Bangkok, Thailand in Bangkapi Government Secondary School.

Marks for the Standard V Examination were as follow:-

Subjects	Marks	Possible marks
Thai	120	69
English	170	124
Social Studies	120	89
Mathematics	240	207
General Science	350	255
Total	1,000	744

Passing grade is 50% of the aggregate marks.

B

KYOTO INSTITUTE OF TECHNOLOGY

Matsugasaki Sakyoku Kyoto 606 JAPAN
Telephone (075) 791-3211   No.1195

Date of Issue: November 6, 1987

C E R T I F I C A T E

Name: ▮▮▮▮▮▮▮▮▮▮

Date of Birth: November 26, 1955

This is to certify that the above mentioned person was admitted to the Department of Architecture of our Faculty on April 14, 1975 and graduated on March 26, 1979 obtaining the Degree of Bachelor of Engineering.

Signature *Susumu Hirase*

(Susumu HIRASE)

Dean
Faculty of Engineering and Design
Kyoto Institute of Technology

Official Seal

C

國 立 政 治 大 學
NATIONAL CHENGCHI UNIVERSITY

TAIPEI, TAIWAN, R. O. C.

Ref. No. 711489   Date: Dec. 23, 1988

TO WHOM IT MAY CONCERN

This is to certify that ▮▮▮▮▮▮▮ (田芳華) ,
a graduate of the Department of ____Education____
College of ____Arts and Sciences____ of this University, was ranked
the ____3rd out of 46____ students in ____her____ class.

Chang Chunhwa

Registrar

Figure 8C. A Sample Transcript

NATIONAL CHIAO TUNG UNIVERSITY
Hsinchu, Taiwan, 300 Republic of China
TRANSCRIPT OF ACADEMIC RECORD

Name   Registration Number   Date Enrolled   August 1983

Department Control Egnineering   Degree Conferred B. S.   June (1987)

Subject of Study	Credits	Grade	Subject of Study	Credits	Grade
Academic Year 1983			Academic Year 1985		
Chinese I,II	4,4	74,77	Automatic Control System I,II	3,3	73,60
English I,II	4,4	77,80	Control Lab.	-,1	--,81
Chinese History I,II	2,2	76,83	The Thoughts of Dr. Sun Yat-Sen	2,2	83,80
Calculus I,II	4,4	77,81	I,II		
Physics I,II	4,4	67,82	Probability and Statistics	3,-	76,--
Physics Lab. I,II	1,1	79,78	Electronics	3,-	82,--
Chemistry I,II	2,2	72,81	Electronics Lab.	1,-	77,--
Chmeistry Lab. I,II	1,1	82,87	Electrical Machinery	3,-	76,--
Computer Programming I,II	2,2	87,79	System Simulation	-,3	--,85
Shop Practice	1,-	85,--	Int. to the Study of Law	-,2	--,80
			Numerical Method and Analysis	-,3	--,90
			Company Law	-,2	--,78
			Practice Project	-,2	--,88
			Electronagnetics	3,-	84,--
			Mechanical Structure and Design	3,-	76,--
			Pneumatic & Hydraulic Control	-,3	--,75
Average (1st Term 1983)	25	75.84	Average (1st Term 1985)	21	78.28
Average (2nd Term 1983)	24	80.46	Average (2nd Term 1985)	21	79.19
Military Training I,II	0,0	80,89			
Physical Education I,II	0,0	71,76	Physical Education I,II	0,0	71,73
Academic Year 1984			Academic Year 1986		
Measurement and Instrumentation	-,3	--,69	Control Lab.	1,-	86,--
Modern Chinese History	-,2	--,70	Digital Control System	3,-	80,--
Engineering Mathematics I,II	3,3	86,78	Int. to Business	-,3	--,91
Int. to Circuit Theory	3,-	81,--	Int. to Modern Control	-,3	--,86
Electronics I,II	3,3	86,80	System Identification	3,-	85,--
Electronics Lab. I,II	1,1	90,92	Control System Design Project	2,-	84,--
Graphics	2,-	77,--	Digital Signal Processing	-,3	--,79
Linear Algebra	3,-	74,--	Stochastic Process	3,-	76,--
Microcomputer System Lab.	-,1	--,78			
Microcomputer System	-,3	--,81			
Microcomputer Lab.	1,-	74,--			
Int. to Control	1,-	80,--			
Int. to Social Science	-,2	--,87			
Int. to Microcomputer	2,-	92,--			
Network Analysis and Synthesis	-,3	--,72			
Japanese	2,-	78,--			
Average (1st Term 1984)	21	81.85	Average (1st Term 1986)	12	81.41
Average (2nd Term 1984)	21	77.33	Average (2nd Term 1986)	9	85.33
Military Training I,II	0,0	80,81			
Physical Education I,II	0,0	79,77	Physical Education I,II	0,0	74,67

60 is the passing grade Below 60=F 60 to 69=C 70 to 79=B 80 or more=A

This transcript is certified as correct according to the record of the University   Date issued JUN 2 3 1988

Dean of Studies   Registrar

When admissions officers look at transcripts, they

1. Compare the information given in the application with what is provided in the academic record

2. Examine records carefully to make sure they are official. If something seems wrong, they may consult an expert to determine the truth of the records.

3. Check to see if the academic background of the applicant has prepared him or her for the program of study at the U.S. university

4. See whether the applicant has completed his or her prior studies

5. Judge whether the applicant has been a successful student

6. Use their experience to judge the quality of the schools that the student has attended

If you are applying to eight universities, you will need eight original transcripts—one for each university you are applying to.

Remember, you must provide a transcript from *each* school you attended if you listed it on your application. If you attended 3 different universities and are applying to 8 U.S. universities, you will need 24 transcripts!!

Practice

EXERCISE 8-2

Compare the information on academic records in Figures 8B and 8C. Then answer the questions.

1. Which academic record shows that the student has a bachelor's degree in engineering?

2. Which academic records include the student's birthdate for identification purposes?

3. Which academic record shows the student's rank in class?

4. Which academic record provides evidence that the student completed high school?

5. Which academic record includes a photograph for identification purposes?

6. Which academic record lists the courses and grades of the student?

7. Which academic record is the most complete?

Questions and Answers

What happens if I do not provide transcripts?

You will be notified by the admissions office that you have missing documents. No decision can be made on your admission if you have missing documents.

Sometimes international students provide too much material on nonacademic achievement, but insufficient contextual information to help us judge their achievements within their schools.
    –Coordinator of International Admissions, Competitive Private College

Which is more important—high school grades or high test scores on standardized tests?

Both are important. Admissions committees try to relate your whole academic history to the U.S. educational system. They also take into consideration your command of English.

What if there is a mistake in my transcript?

Look at your transcripts to make sure they are correct. If you have had them translated, check over the translation. Make sure the dates and marks are correct.

How do I know how to translate the name of my degree?

Do not translate a degree into its U.S. name. Use the degree names used in your country.

There are some special terms in my language, and it's difficult to find equivalent words in English.–*Student*

My teacher translated my forms. What if he made a mistake?

Admissions officers check your forms very carefully. They are looking for students who

- Add subjects or increase grades on documents
- Place their own name over another name on a certificate
- Fill in details on a counterfeit certificate

They are also looking for missing information, gaps, and mistakes in translation. For example, the original document of an Argentinian student said "Licenciado en Ciencia Politica." The English translation said "Master's in Political Science." These terms are not equivalent. Admissions officers realize that most students are *not* trying to deceive them and will write to you for clarification.

There are serious consequences, however, for deliberately "altered documents": They send you a rejection letter, with copies to

- Your parents
- Your school
- Your examination board
- The U.S. Immigration and Naturalization Service
- Your embassy

ARRANGING FOR REFERENCES/LETTERS OF RECOMMENDATION

In the previous sections we've looked at how the application form asks for information on your family, your education, your jobs, and your examination results in order to get a "picture" of you as a student and as a person. Another way to learn more about you is to read a letter of recommendation or reference from someone who knows you well as a student and as a person. Your teacher, your professor, your counselor, or your principal will usually write one for you. Sometimes a university asks for a "peer recommendation"—this is a recommendation from another student. All recommendations answer the same questions: Are you a good student? Are you an interesting person?

Often there is a special form that may have

- A list of questions
- A series of boxes to be checked
- One general question

Think about who knows you well and can write about your recent work and assess your potential. Ask your reference well in advance—writing a letter of reference is a lot of work and may take some time. It's a good idea to tell your reference about your academic plans and about the places you would like to study. This information will make the task of writing about you a little easier.

If you are applying for graduate studies, recommendations should come from professors who know you well and can give details on your research and academic experiences. If they are respected figures in the field, of course it is much more helpful! Your professors will be asked to give details of your

research and academic qualifications

writing skills

professionalism

emotional stability

work relationships

probability of success

Give your professors your own notes about all of the above, and also your résumé, so that they can do the recommendations easily.

Of course, we are all curious to know what is written about us. In the United States there is a law that gives people the right to see the information in files. On reference forms there is often a *waiver*—you can *waive* (give up) your right to see the letter written about you. (You can still look at the rest of your file.) It's probably a good idea to sign the waiver. Sometimes teachers and professors write in only very general terms when they know the student is going to see the letter. Admissions officers may interpret a recommendation with a waiver as more honest.

Figure 8D on the next page shows the recommendation sections from three forms and the waiver from another.

Figure 8D. Three Reference (Recommendation) Sections and a Waiver

A

23 LIST THREE PERSONS ACQUAINTED WITH YOUR ACADEMIC EXPERIENCES WHOM YOU HAVE REQUESTED TO SEND LETTERS OF REFERENCE TO THE DESIGNATED DEPARTMENT OR PROGRAM.
(Not Required For Special Standing)

NAME	POSITION	ADDRESS

24 INDICATE THE FOLLOWING TESTS TAKEN   GMAT

B

4. Recommendation letter(s): Beginning undergraduates—One from the principal or headmaster of the last school attended. Advanced undergraduates—One from your adviser or major professor. Graduates—Three from major professors and/or other colleagues. (These same three letters may also be used in support of a fellowship or assistantship application.) At least two of the letters should be from major professors at the institution you last attended or currently attend. The letters should be written on letterhead stationery.

C

References: Please list the names and addresses of at least three persons, preferably professors or professionals under whom you have studied.

NAME	ADDRESS	PHONE NUMBER	POSITION

D

10. (Optional) I hereby waive my rights of access to this confidential recommendation as provided in the Educational Rights and Privacy Act of 1974.

Signature_____ Date_____

Instructions to the applicant: Items 1-9 **must** be completed; you may sign item 10 if you wish to waive your right of access to this letter. Give this form to a person who is well acquainted with your education and abilities.

Instructions to the writer: Below please state your opinion of the applicant's ability to carry on advanced study and research, teaching potential, and capacity to pursue a successful career in his or her field. Use the reverse side if necessary. Mail the form directly to the executive officer and department specified above. If the applicant has signed item 10 above, the confidentiality of this letter of reference is assured.

Practice

EXERCISE 8-3

Ask one of your classmates to write a peer recommendation, a letter about you as a student and as a person. Offer to do the same for him or her. Read and discuss your opinions and use this as a source for your notes for your teacher, or ideas for your statement of purpose.

EXERCISE 8-4

Read the following questions that appear on forms for references. Answer these questions about yourself. Imagine you are writing a reference for someone else. Make a list of the main points of the information on yourself. Use this in a discussion with, or to give to, your reference.

1. How long have you known the applicant?
2. What is your relationship to the applicant?
3. What do you consider the applicant's main academic interests, abilities, and weaknesses to be?
4. Please give a brief statement about the applicant's personality, involvement in school and community activities, and leadership potential.
5. Are there any factors that might prevent this student from developing his or her full potential for academic and personal growth in college?
6. Additional remarks.

Questions and Answers

I'm applying to graduate school. My favorite teacher was Mr. Li. He taught me English when I was 14. Should I ask him for a letter of recommendation?

Probably not. You really need someone who has taught you recently in the subject you want to study. Remember—your academic work is the most important part of your application. However, a letter of recommendation about your English proficiency is useful, and some universities request this.

Professor Askari is very well known and I had good grades in her classes, but she is very busy. Should I ask her for a reference?

Yes, but ask her well in advance. Give her as much information as you can so that she can write the reference easily. Then later, politely check whether she has done it. It's important to make sure that your reference is someone who will write the letter on time!

UNDERSTANDING THE VISA PROCESS

For many students, getting a visa is sometimes a very frustrating experience.

Why did you, officials in the graduate school, send the I-20 so late? I had so much difficulty getting a passport and visa. I think you have to send the I-20 form as soon as possible.–*Student*

In the application form the university wants to collect as much information from you as possible at one time, and therefore the form will often have questions about citizenship, passports, etc. This is because later, when the university offers you a place, it is easy to get this information from the files or computer to authorize the documents for a visa for you. The university is required by the Immigration and Naturalization Service (INS) to maintain this information until you leave the university. Fill in the information accurately, and let the university know if there are any changes in your situation—for example, if you apply for permanent residency in the United States, or if you marry and wish to bring your spouse.

Remember that you cannot go to the United States on a visitor's visa and then get a visa to study there. When your university admission is confirmed, you will receive a form from the university, and you take this to the nearest U.S. consulate for a visa. There are different forms to send for each type of student visa:

- With an I-20 form you get a F-1 student visa—for full-time students
- With an IAP-66 form you get a J-1 exchange visitor visa—for sponsored students

Students at technical schools get an M visa, and they can't change to an F-1 visa. However, a student with an F-1 visa could change to an M visa.

With an F-1 visa it is possible to stay after you have finished your degree for up to one year while doing practical training; with an M visa, for up to six months; with a J-1 visa, for up to 18 months—if training is necessary and not available at home, and if your sponsor agrees.

At the consulate a visa officer will check your documents and decide if you are eligible. This decision will be based on factors other than academic records. Among other things, the visa officer will consider whether you will return after you finish your studies.

Many state universities will ask you if you are a *resident* of that state, and how long you have lived there. If you live in a state for over a year and it is your "domicile" you may be eligible for the in-state tuition fee. You may not claim to have a domicile in the United States on a *student* visa, however.

Practice

EXERCISE 8-5

Read about the four students on page 126. Match each student with his or her form (Figure 8E) by writing *A, B,* or *C* after each description. One student's form is not shown. (See the form in Exercise 8-6).

Figure 8E. Three Students' Residency Responses

A

Visa Status

☐ Student Visa (F-1)   ☐ Exchange Visitor (J-1)

☐ Visitor Visa (B-2)   ☐ Other Visa (_____)

Country of Citizenship:

Vietnam

Permanent U.S. Status

☐ U.S. Citizen

☐ Immigrant

Social Security Number

A-21-172-056

Alien Registration Number

Are you a Michigan resident? ☑ Yes   ☐ No

If yes, how long? *5 years 8 months* (years/months)

B

22 ARE YOU A U.S. CITIZEN?	23 WHAT IS YOUR COUNTRY OF CITIZENSHIP?	UC USE ONLY	24 WHAT IS YOUR COUNTRY OF PERMANENT RESIDENCE?
(1) ☐ YES — SKIP TO ITEM 30 (2) ☑ NO	B R A Z I L		VENEZUELA

25 IF NOT A U.S. CITIZEN, WHAT IS YOUR STATUS?

(1) ☐ IMMIGRANT/(PR) PERMANENT U.S. RESIDENT — GO TO ITEM 27

(2) ☐ (RF) REFUGEE — GO TO ITEM 27

(3) ☑ NONIMMIGRANT — CONTINUE WITH ITEM 26

26 IF NONIMMIGRANT, WHAT TYPE OF VISA DO YOU HOLD, HAVE YOU APPLIED FOR, OR DO YOU PLAN TO APPLY FOR?

(1) ☐ (A) DIPLOMATIC (2) ☐ (F1) STUDENT (3) ☐ (F2) STUDENT SPOUSE

(4) ☑ (J1) EXCHANGE (5) ☐ (J2) EXCHANGE — VISITOR SPOUSE

(6) ☐ OTHER   PLEASE SPECIFY:

C

SECTION D—RESIDENCY INFORMATION

You are responsible for providing correct information about your visa status and residency. Failure to answer these questions completely may result in your being classified incorrectly for visa or tuition purposes. Additional documentation may be required as is deemed necessary by the university.

Are you a U.S. citizen? ⟶ yes ☐ no ☑

If no, what type of visa do you hold or will you hold? *F-1*

What is the country of your birth? *Sri Lanka*

What is the country of your citizenship? *Pakistan*

Are you a permanent resident or refugee? ⟶ yes ☐ no ☑

What is your alien registration number? _____ Date_____

Applicants who hold an E, G, or A visa may qualify for in-state tuition. See admissions officer for further details.

Are you claiming Texas as your place of domicile and that you are now eligible for in-state tuition? ⟶ yes ☐ no ☑

1 VISA 2 COUNTRY 3 RES 4 TS

1. Manique was born in Sri Lanka and now lives in and is a citizen of Pakistan. She wants to be a full-time student.

2. Lon Tran is from Vietnam. She is an immigrant and has lived in Grand Rapids, Michigan, for five years. Her alien registration number is A-21-172-056.

3. Ivan is Brazilian. His family moved to Venezuela three years ago. He has worked in Venezuela for one year, and his company will sponsor him to study in the United States. He likes the United States, but plans to return to Brazil to work.

4. Eugenia Stetlovovitch is from Leningrad, USSR, where she was born. Her government is sending her to the United States to get her Ph.D.

EXERCISE 8-6

Fill in this form for the fourth student.

5. NAME			6. DATE OF BIRTH	7. MALE FEMALE
LAST FIRST MIDDLE/FORMER SURNAME			MO | DAY | YR |	☐ ☐

8. REQUIRED FOR FEDERAL REPORTING BY CIVIL RIGHTS ACT OF 1964
   1 CAUCASIAN WHITE   3 ASIAN OR PACIFIC ISLANDER   5 HISPANIC
RACE (CHECK ONE) 2 BLACK NEGRO 4 AMERICAN INDIAN OR ALASKAN NATIVE 6 OTHER FOREIGN STUDENT

9. ARE YOU A CITIZEN OF THE UNITED STATES?	IF NO, INDICATE	10. BIRTHPLACE
YES NO	COUNTRY VISA STATUS	COUNTY STATE COUNTRY
☐ ☐		

Questions and Answers

I want to mail my forms because it is almost the deadline, but my passport has expired. I have applied for a new one. What should I do?

Send your application form immediately—you must not miss the deadline! On the form write clearly "I applied for a new passport on _____ (date). I will send you this information when I receive it." Always make a copy of your passport before you mail it.

I am single. I plan to study in the United States for a year, come home to get married, and then take my spouse back to the United States with me for my second year of studies. What should I put on the form?

Answer the questions as they apply to your situation *now*. Your plans may change. When you marry you may have to fill in different forms for visas and housing.

The international admissions office won't send me the I-20 until I have proof of my scholarship, but my sponsors won't sign until I have the I-20. What can I do?

It's best to work something out with your sponsors. They are nearer, and you know them better! Furthermore, a university cannot legally send you the I-20 until it has proof of your financial circumstances. The university will send you the I-20 as soon as it has this proof.

FINISHING UP

Signing the form is the easiest thing to do, but admissions officers say you would be surprised at how many students forget to do so! If the form is not signed, they cannot process your application. They will send it back to you, and this will certainly delay your application. And remember that a photocopy of your signature is not acceptable, so make sure you have actually signed the form you send.

Don't forget! Please sign, and date, the form!

Above the signature, there are a few lines that form a *contract*. They begin with the words "I certify" or "I understand" or "I agree." In general, by signing the statement you are saying that you have told the truth on the forms—"the information is correct and complete"—and that you will obey the rules of the university.

Sometimes, the statement asks you to say that you understand certain other things—for example, that there may be an increase in costs. And that if you have not told the truth, you can be dismissed from the university. Some examples are shown in Figure 8F. It is important to be able to understand the consequences of signing the form and recognize and understand legal terms. Basically, the contract says that if they find a lie

- Before you're admitted, they won't admit you
- After you're admitted, they may expel you

Practice

EXERCISE 8-7

Look at the forms in Figure 8F on the next page. Then answer the questions by writing *A, B, C,* or *D*.

1. Which was the easiest to understand?
2. Which asks you to print your name?
3. Which mention finances?
4. Which mention penalties for lying?

8F. The Signature

A _____   _____   _____

I certify that all the answers on this application are complete and accurate to the best of my knowledge. I have also read carefully the costs of enrollment and am prepared to meet these expenses.

Signature *Wei-Mei Wong* _____ Date *Sept. 5, 1992*

B _____

23. I understand that withholding information requested on this application or giving false information may make me ineligible for admission to the University. With this in mind, I certify that the above statements are correct and complete.

_____*Ahmed Jamal*_____   _____*Oct 12, 1992*_____
signature (do not print)   date

C

An application fee of $25 (check or money order payable to BGSU) ***must accompany this application.*** This application fee is nonrefundable. ***Please do not send cash.***

*In accordance with the Right of Privacy Act of 1974, Public Law 93-x579, Sect. 7, applicants for admission are requested to voluntarily report their Social Security number on this form. The number is used for identification and record keeping purposes. BGSU is an equal opportunity/affirmative action employer.

I certify the information hereon is complete, accurate and true to the best of my knowledge. I understand that any misrepresentation of facts hereon will be cause for refusal of admission, cancellation of admission or expulsion from the University if discovered subsequently. I agree that as a student I am subject to the Student Code of Bowling Green State University.

Mail this application to: Office of Admissions, Bowling Green State University, Bowling Green, Ohio 43403

signature _____*Hiromi Shoji*_____   date _____*Jan 3, 1993*_____
                                                              (continued on reverse side)

D

XII. YOUR SIGNATURE—ALL APPLICANTS
95	**IMPORTANT: Your signature is required below. Without your signature, your application is not complete.**

I certify that I have considered each question carefully and that my statements are true and complete to the best of my knowledge. Further, I understand that admission to or enrollment in the University of California may be denied if any information is found to be incomplete or inaccurate.

SIGNATURE OF APPLICANT (In ink)	DATE OF APPLICATION
Linda Paterson	*November 1, 1992*

Questions and Answers

Do I sign my name in my own script or in English?

Write your signature in English, as this is how you will sign all official documents once you arrive in the United States. You must write, not print, for a signature.

I would never tell a lie on my application form, but signing the contract makes me nervous. What if I made a mistake?

Obviously, if it is a genuine mistake, the university will try to clarify it and be sympathetic to your explanation. Many contracts also include the phrase "to the best of my knowledge." This means that when you sign, you believe at that time that everything written on the form is true.

MIT photo by Calvin Campbell, courtesy of Massachusetts Institute of Technology

Follow-up Correspondence

- ► DID I FORGET TO SEND SOMETHING?

- ► DID I GET IN?

- ► WRITING LETTERS OF ACCEPTANCE AND REFUSAL

DID I FORGET TO SEND SOMETHING?

After you send your application and all the documents to the university, the university will send a letter telling you that your application has been received.

Did you send everything you needed to send?

The admissions officers will check to make sure your application is complete. Remember the checklist? Admissions officers will also use a checklist to make sure they have everything they need from you.

The university will notify you if your application is incomplete, but some missing documents may delay the processing of your application.

The university will keep your records on a computer file. It is important that the information (sometimes called data in computer language) is correct.

After the university receives your application, you may be sent a list of information about yourself. Check it carefully to see that it is correct. It is especially important that your name is correct and that the information shows the program you want to enter.

If an applicant wants financial aid, it is very important that the file be complete. We can't send the file to the department until we get the student's transcripts and test scores.–*Admissions Officer, Large University*

Some students ask us to waive the application fee. Some universities do that, but we don't automatically do that unless the circumstances are very special. We do not review the file until we get the application fee.–*Graduate Admissions Officer*

Practice

EXERCISE 9-1

Figure 9A shows a card sent to a student who has applied to a university. The applicant must verify that the information is correct. If there are mistakes, she corrects them and returns the card to the university. If all the information is correct, she does not need to return the card. In this case, the applicant found some mistakes. Notice how she corrected the information.

Answer the following questions.

1. What kind of visa does she want?
2. When does she want to begin her studies?
3. Is the information about her major area of study correct?
4. Is the level of study correct?
5. What is her Social Security number?

Figure 9A. Application Verification Form

Name: Wei Mei WONG

Assigned Student ID: P79-13-1942
Birthdate: 06-11-70
Residency: NON-MICHIGAN
Geog. Location: Taiwan
Visa: ~~Exchange Visitor~~ F-1 Student Visa
Country of Birth: ~~Thailand~~ Taiwan

Term/Year: Fall 94 / 93
Entry Type: 4

Unit: 3510
Field: 2580 ECONOMICS

Program Level: ~~Master's~~ Ph.D.

Mailing address:
3G No 3 Alley 18 Lane 25
Soshing North Street
Taipei, Taiwan ROC

Questions and Answers

What should I do if I do not receive an acknowledgment letter from a university that I apply to?

You should write and ask whether your application was received. Be sure to include your name, birthdate, and the date that you mailed it. Some students who live in countries with irregular mail service send their applications by registered mail.

DID I GET IN?

An applicant's file is reviewed for

- academic qualifications
- English proficiency
- financial resources

Sometimes an applicant is academically qualified and has financial resources, but the student's background and test scores suggest that the student needs higher English proficiency to succeed in an academic program. This situation is likely to result in conditional acceptance, the status of the student who received the letter in Figure 9B.

Figure 9B.   A Letter of Conditional Acceptance

Wayne State University

Thank you for submitting an application for admission to Wayne State University.

It is our pleasure to report that your academic background does make you eligible for admission to this institution. However, since you do not meet our requirement for English language proficiency, it will be necessary that you initially attend and successfully complete an intensive English language program at the Wayne State University English Language Institute. The determination of your success in that program will be made by the score you achieve on the English language examination, which is administered at the end of the program. Once the examination has been passed, you will be granted admission to Wayne State University as a fully matriculated student in _____the College of Engineering_____.

Enclosed is a Certificate of Eligibility (Form I-20) for the Wayne State University English Language Institute. This must be presented to the nearest United States Consul in order to secure your student visa.

If you have any questions, please feel free to call this office at (313) 555-3577, or the Wayne State University English Language Institute at (313) 555-2729.

Sincerely,

International Student Counselor

Enclosure

Practice

EXERCISE 9-2

Read Figure 9B and then answer the following questions.

1. Is a student who receives this letter admitted to the university?
2. What must the student do before she can begin her academic study at the university?
3. What score is needed on the English language examination?
4. What is a student called who is admitted and enrolled in a regular academic program?
5. Did this student meet the financial requirements of the university? What are your reasons for your answer?
6. What is the certificate of eligibility for?
7. How long will the student need to study English before she will be admitted to an academic program?

Questions and Answers

Can a student use an I-20 from one university to attend another university?

No, the I-20 is a form that shows that a student may be eligible for an F-1 visa. Another university can issue a student another I-20. The university that issues the I-20 expects the student to study there for at least one term.

My friend was admitted last year to a university with a TOEFL score of 540. He was admitted to a regular academic program. I applied to the same university this year and was only admitted conditionally. My TOEFL score was about the same. I don't think it's fair. I've written to the admissions office and told them about my friend.

Each admission is a separate decision. The admissions committee have reasons for their decision. If you think a mistake has been made, explain the situation to the admissions office. If you have a more recent, higher test score, make sure that the admissions office has the new score in your file.

Apply to several universities. If you are not accepted at the university of your first choice, you may be accepted at one of your other choices. You can attend the other university, and then you may be able to transfer to your first choice the next year if you do well in your U.S. studies.

I applied for undergraduate (freshman) study at a large state university. I received a letter saying I am wait-listed. What does that mean? Is that the same as conditionally admitted?

No. If you are on the waiting list, you may or may not be allowed to enroll. The university had too many qualified applicants. If some of the students already offered admission decide not to enroll, then the university may offer you a place. Smaller colleges and universities also wait-list students.

In general, international applicants to large state universities should apply as early as possible. State universities reserve a certain number of places for nonresident students—and international students are considered nonresident students. When these places are filled, the university will not accept additional students.

I was admitted for the fall term, but my mother is going to have an operation in August and I want to stay home with her. What should I do? Do I have to apply all over again if I do not attend in the fall?

No. You should write to the university and explain your situation. You could ask if you could delay your admission until the winter term. This is called delaying matriculation. A delay may be possible in some programs.

WRITING LETTERS OF ACCEPTANCE AND REFUSAL

If you receive a "thick" envelope from the university, you can probably start celebrating! Universities often send a lot of other information—on such matters as housing, orientation, transportation, and health care—with your letter of acceptance. But what if you get two, or more, acceptances? Making a decision on which university to attend is hard. Now is the time to review all the points you raised at the beginning of the job of applying to a U.S. university. Are the courses of study, the reputation, the financial aid award, the location, the climate, etc. still of the same importance to you?

You will probably have to make a decision fairly quickly. Note any deadline mentioned in the acceptance letter. Write a letter to your final choice accepting the offer, and send a copy of that letter to the international student advisor at the university. Next, it is customary and courteous to write a polite letter to the other universities explaining that you do not plan to enroll, as you will be attending another school. If you do this, the universities can go ahead and make an offer to the next person on the waiting list. Figure 9C shows the placement of the parts of a letter of acceptance or refusal.

Practice

EXERCISE 9-3

Zhou Jie-wen has been accepted by two universities. She has decided to refuse Midwest University and accept Southern University. She took notes on how to write an acceptance and a refusal letter, but the notes are mixed up. Complete the two letters, the accepting letter and the refusing letter, with the right sentences in the right order. Some of the sentences can be placed in both letters.

a. I understand that I must take an Academic English Evaluation. I will report to the Intensive English Program as soon as I arrive.

b. I enclose the $100.00 (one hundred dollars) confirming deposit as requested.

c. Mary Brown
Director, International Admissions
Southern University
Bigtown, AK 12345
USA

d. I will present the I-20 to the U.S. Embassy in our capital as soon as possible. I plan to travel to the United States on August 25th so that I can arrive in time for the orientation programs. I have noted the dates for the International Student Orientation and the New Student Academic Orientation, and I look forward to attending both.

e. Dear Ms. Brown:

f. Thank you for the information on housing. I understand that I will be in co-educational housing and sharing a room with another student. When you re-

Figure 9C. Form of a Letter of Acceptance or Refusal

ceive my confirming deposit, I look forward to receiving an application form for housing and more information from the Director of Housing on residence halls.

g. Thank you for your letter of March 1st informing me that my application for admission to your university has been approved.

h. Yours sincerely,

i. I regret that I am unable to accept your offer of admission. I will be attending another school.

j. Zhou Jie-wen

k. March 10, 1993

l. James Howard
Associate Director for International Admissions
Midwest University
Midtown, MI 54321
USA

m. 14 Zhong Yuan Street
Zhong Shan District
Dalian
PRC

n. Dear Mr. Howard:

Questions and Answers

I can't decide which place to go to. Can I send my confirming deposit to both universities while I make up my mind?

No! You *cannot* accept two colleges. If you try to do this, you make everything very complicated for the universities. You also prevent other students on the waiting list from having a chance of an offer.

Always remember that if you find on arrival that you have made a mistake—that you really don't like the university, courses, teachers, weather, or whatever!—you can try to transfer to another university after one semester. However, transferring means that you have to go through the application process again.

APPENDIXES

APPENDIX 1

Names in the United States

1. The standard name form is first, or given, name; middle name or middle initial; and then last, or family, name. Some examples are

   John Davis Anderson
   John D. Anderson
   Susan Ann White
   Susan A. White

   Several terms can be used to describe names.
   Family name = Surname = Last Name   **Anderson**
   Given name = First Name   **John**
   Middle name = Second given name   **Davis**
   MI = middle initial   **D.**

2. You will usually be required to print your last name *first* on forms and applications

   Anderson   John   D.
   _____
   (last name)   (first name)   (MI)

3. When you write your signature, however, you use the standard name form.

   John   D.   Anderson
   _____
   (first name)   (MI)   (last name)

4. An international applicant should make it clear which name is his or her last name and which name is his or her first name by

   - underlining his or her family name
     <u>Xu</u> Wihan   Wihan <u>Xu</u>
   - using uppercase capitals for his or her family name
     XU Wihan   Wihan XU

APPENDIX 2

Undergraduate Applicants to Community Colleges

There are approximately 1,000 community colleges in the United States. Sometimes called junior colleges, these two-year colleges have more flexible admission requirements than four-year colleges and universities.

About thirteen percent of all international students in the United States attend community colleges. Community colleges located in areas with many international students and nonnative speakers of English, such as California, southern Florida, or New York, often have ESL (English as a Second Language) classes for international students. Not all community colleges require international students to take academic entrance tests. They usually do, however, require applicants to take English language tests before accepting them for study.

Most community colleges are designed to serve the educational and job needs of a community and are publicly operated with city or local county tax funds. These two-year colleges do not offer residence facilities—places to live—on campus.

The highest degree offered by a community college is an associate degree. Students can receive an A.A., Associate of Arts, degree or an A.S., Associate of Science, degree.

A student may transfer from a community college to a four-year college or university. The credits earned at the community college can frequently be transferred toward a bachelor's degree at the four-year institution. The reputation of the community college and the student's academic record are used by the four-year college to determine his or her academic qualifications. Students who transfer from community colleges in the United States usually do not have to provide test scores to the four-year universities.

Community colleges have smaller application fees. Tuition fees for residents of the community that the two-year college serves are generally much less than at four-year colleges. Tuition fees are higher, however, for *all* nonresidents of a community, including international students.

When a student requests information from a community college, the college will send information brochures along with various admissions forms. Because the brochures and forms are usually prepared for students already living in the community, the information may be confusing to an international student. If you have questions, write to the college.

APPENDIX 3

U.S. Universities with the Most International Students

International students are enrolled at ninety percent of American universities. Some universities have only a few international students while others have hundreds of international students.

Each of the following American universities has more than 1,000 international students. The universities are organized by geographical regions in the United States.

Name of university	City, State, Zip
NORTHEAST	
Boston University	Boston, MA 02215
City University of New York-Baruch College	New York, NY 10010
City University of New York-City College	New York, NY 10013
Columbia University	New York, NY 10027
Cornell University	Ithaca, NY 14853
Harvard University	Cambridge, MA 02138
Massachusetts Institute of Technology	Cambridge, MA 02139
New Jersey Institute of Technology	Newark, NJ 07102
New York University	New York, NY 10003
Northeastern University	Boston, MA 02115
Pennsylvania State University	University Park, PA 16802
Rutgers University	New Brunswick, NJ 08903
State University of New York-Buffalo	Buffalo, NY 14214
State University of New York-Stony Brook	Stony Brook, NY 11794
Syracuse University	Syracuse, NY 13210
Temple University	Philadelphia, PA 19122
University of Massachusetts at Amherst	Amherst, MA 01003
University of Pennsylvania	Philadelphia, PA 19119
University of Pittsburgh	Pittsburgh, PA 15260
Yale University	New Haven, CT 06520

SOUTH/SOUTHEAST	
American University	Washington, DC 20016
Florida International University	Miami, FL 33199
Florida State University	Tallahassee, FL 32306
Georgetown University	Washington, DC 20057
George Washington University	Washington, DC 20052
Georgia State University	Atlanta, GA 30303
Howard University	Washington, DC 20059
Jackson State University	Jackson, MS 39217
Louisiana State University	Baton Rouge, LA 70803
Miami-Dade Community College	Miami, FL 33167
North Carolina State University	Raleigh, NC 27650
Northern Virginia Community College	Annandale, VA 22003
Southern University of A&M College	Baton Rouge, LA 70813
Virginia Polytechnic and State University	Blacksburg, VA 24061
University of District of Columbia	Washington, DC 20008
University of Florida	Gainesville, FL 32611
University of Georgia	Athens, GA 30602
University of Maryland-College Park	College Park, MD 20742
University of Miami	Coral Gables, FL 33124

SOUTHWEST	
Arizona State University	Tempe, AZ 85287
Oklahoma State University	Stillwater, OK 74078
Texas A&M University	College Station, TX 77843
Texas Southern University	Houston, TX 77004a
University of Arizona	Tucson, AZ 85721
University of Houston	Houston, TX 77004
University of North Texas	Denton, TX 76203
University of Oklahoma	Norman, OK 73019
University of Texas-Arlington	Arlington, TX 76019
University of Texas-Austin	Austin, TX 78712

MIDWEST

Eastern Michigan University	Ypsilanti, MI 48197
Indiana University-Bloomington	Bloomington, IN 47405
Iowa State University	Ames, IA 50011
Purdue University-West Lafayette	West Lafayette, IN 47907
Michigan State University	East Lansing, MI 48824
Ohio University	Athens, OH 45701
Ohio State University-main campus	Columbus, OH 43210
Southern Illinois University at Carbondale	Carbondale, IL 62901
University of Akron	Akron, OH 44325
University of Chicago	Chicago, IL 60637
University of Illinois at Chicago	Chicago, IL 60680
University of Illinois at Urbana-Champaign	Urbana, IL 61801
University of Iowa	Iowa City, IA 52242
University of Kansas	Lawrence, KS 66045
University of Michigan-Ann Arbor	Ann Arbor, MI 48109
University of Minnesota-Twin Cities	Minneapolis, MN 55455
University of Missouri	Columbia, MO 65211
University of Toledo	Toledo, OH 43606
University of Wisconsin-Madison	Madison, WI 53706
Wayne State University	Detroit, MI 48202

PACIFIC-WEST

California State University, Long Beach	Long Beach, CA 90840
California State University, Los Angeles	Los Angeles, CA 90032
Oregon State University	Corvallis, OR 97331
San Francisco State University	San Francisco, CA 94132
Stanford University	Stanford, CA 94305
University of California-Los Angeles	Los Angeles, CA 90024
University of California-Berkeley	Berkeley, CA 94720
University of California-Davis	Davis, CA 95616
University of California-San Diego	La Jolla, CA 92093
University of Hawaii-Manoa	Honolulu, HI 96822
University of Oregon	Eugene, OR 97403
University of Southern California	Los Angeles, CA 90089
University of Washington	Seattle, WA 98195

Source: *Open Doors 1989-90: Report on International Educational Exchange*. New York: Institute for International Education, 1990.

MOUNTAIN-WEST

Brigham Young University	Provo, UT 84602
University of Utah	Salt Lake City, UT 88112

APPENDIX 4
Sample Graduate Application for Admission (Page 1 of 3)

The University of Michigan
Horace H. Rackham
School of Graduate Studies
Ann Arbor, Michigan 48109-1070
U.S.A.

INTERNATIONAL STUDENT
APPLICATION FOR ADMISSION

This application is for non-U.S. citizens.

$30 Application Fee must be attached.

_____ Check here if you are submitting
more than one application.

PLEASE PRINT OR TYPE

1. Have you ever applied for admission to Rackham Graduate School? ☒ No   ☐ Yes _____
   Term   Year   School/College

2. Do you have a U.S. Social Security Number?   ☒ No   ☐ Yes ☐☐☐ - ☐☐ - ☐☐☐☐
   U.S. Social Security Number

3. Full Name ___Li_____ ___Sheng-Kuei_____ _____ _____
   Last/Family Name/Surname   First/Given   Middle   Please list former names which may
                                                                                     appear on transcripts being submitted.

4. Permanent Address   Valid until __1/31/99__
   __35, Ln 180, Sec. 6_____
   Address line 1
   __San Hoc Road   San Chung_____
   Address line 2
   __Taipei, Taiwan   ROC   10605_____
   City, State/Country, Mail/Zip Code
   Telephone __886 2 9991111___ ___886 2 8885432___
            Day (Area Code/Number)   Night (Area Code/Number)

   Electronic Mail Address _____

5. Mailing Address, if different   Valid until _____
   _____
   Address line 1
   _____
   Address line 2
   _____
   City, State/Country, Mail/Zip Code
   Telephone _____ _____
            Day (Area Code/Number)   Night (Area Code/Number)

   Valid Until _____

6. Sex __X__ Male _____ Female

7. Country of Citizenship __Taiwan   ROC_____

8. Birth Date __5/31/66__
            Month/Day/Year

9. Birthplace __Nantou, Taiwan ROC_____
            City/Country

10. Program Name __Industrial & Operations Engineering__   Code ☐4☐3☐9☐2☐
    (Code number follows program name on pages 16-31)

11. Subfield __Management Engineering__

12. Program level for which you are applying
    (check one)

    __X__ 23 Master's
    Do you plan to continue for Doctoral
    program?
    _____ Yes _____ No __X__ Undecided

    _____ 28 Certificate

    _____ 24 Professional (Specialist)

    _____ 25 Doctoral Program

    _____ 20 Not-Candidate for a Degree

13. Term of proposed enrollment
    (check one)

    _____ 913 Winter January 1991

    _____ 914 Spring May 1991

    _____ 921 Summer Half July 1991

    __X__ 922 Fall September 1991

    _____ 923 Winter January 1992

14. Location of proposed enrollment
    (check one)

    __X__ A106 Ann Arbor Campus

    _____ D130 Dearborn Campus

    _____ F142 Flint Campus

    Be sure the program you selected is
    offered at the campus you checked.
    See pages 16-31.

15. Previous Education. List, in chronological order, all post-secondary institutions attended. You must submit official credentials and translations in
    duplicate from all institutions listed below. Do not translate degree names. (Note: Your application will not be reviewed until the credentials are
    received.)

Institution	Location — please list: City, State/Country	Attended from Mo/Yr	Attended until Mo/Yr	Major Field	Name of Degree or Diploma received/expected	Date received or expected Mo/Yr
National Chiao Tung University	Hsinchu, Taiwan	8/84	6/88	Marine Engineering	B.S.E.	6/88

SPACE BELOW FOR RACKHAM USE ONLY:

OTD   TO WHOM   DELP   DFRS   DF&E   VISA _____   HS _____

PR/PL   and   apnd   epnd   I-20   IAP-66

A b 1 2 3 4 5 6 7 8 9   TOEFL/MELAB _____   UPGPA _____   GRGPA _____

1070/0490

Sample Graduate Application for Admission   (Page 2 of 3)

16. Visa Status: Please read the Passports and Visas section of the accompanying brochure (page 11) and then supply the information requested below:

Applicants currently **outside** the U.S.A.

a. What type of visa do you plan to obtain?

- ☒ F-1 Student
- ☐ J-1 Exchange Visitor
- ☐ Other _____

b. If you are applying for the J-1 visa, do you wish The University of Michigan to issue the IAP-66 Certificate?

- ☐ Yes   ☐ No

c. If no, write the name of the agency or institution issuing your IAP-66 Certificate.

_____

_____

_____

Applicants currently **in** the U.S.A.

a. What type of visa do you currently hold?

- ☐ F-1 Student
  - INS Admission No. _____
- ☐ J-1 Exchange Visitor
- ☐ Other _____

b. Do you intend to hold the same type of visa while studying at The University of Michigan?

- ☐ Yes   ☐ No

c. If no, indicate the status you intend to hold.

- ☐ F-1 Student
- ☐ J-1 Exchange Visitor
- ☐ Permanent Resident Alien Reg. No. _____
- ☐ Other _____

17. Number of dependents (spouse and/or children) you intend to bring to the U.S.A. and support during your studies: Please give requested information for each dependent below.

Name	Relationship	Country of Birth	Birthdate

18. Confidential Statement of Finances

Source of Funds	Yearly Amounts (in U.S. dollars)				Total Amount for All Years
	1st	2nd	3rd	4th	
Personal Savings*	$ 25,000	$	$	$	$ 25,000
Parental Support*	$	$ 27,000	$	$	$ 27,000
Scholarship (indicate name of sponsor)*	$	$	$	$	$
Other Sources*	$	$	$	$	$
Yearly Totals	$ 25,000	$ 27,000	$	$	$ 52,000

*All personal and parental funds listed above must be documented by bank statements and letters of support; funding from scholarships and other sources must be documented by official letters stating the amounts of funding available and for what period of time. *PLEASE NOTE:* photostatic copies are *NOT* acceptable.

19. Are you applying for a financial award from the program?   ____ Yes   X̲ No

If yes, write to the department/program directly. *THIS FORM IS NOT AN APPLICATION FOR FINANCIAL ASSISTANCE.*

Sample Graduate Application for Admission   (Page 3 of 3)

20. Persons submitting letters of recommendation, if any. Ask recommenders to use your full name as it appears on your application.

Name	Title	Institution/Company/Location
Li-Min Tsai	Chairman	Dept. of Marine Engineering National Chiao Tung University, Hsinchu
Hung-Nan Lin	Professor	same as above
Yishu Hsieh	Deputy Director	Dept. of Marine Protection Public Utilities Board Taipei

21. Employment and Experience: List, in chronological order, all relevant employment and work experience since secondary school graduation.

a. Employer: Public Utilities Board   Location: Taipei, Taiwan

Dates of Employment: from mo./yr. 7/90 to mo./yr. present   Position: Inspection Engineer

b. Employer: ROC Army (military service)   Location: Long Fei Island

Dates of Employment: from mo./yr. 7/88 to mo./yr. 6/90   Position: 2nd Lieutenant

c. Employer: _____   Location: _____

Dates of Employment: from mo./yr. _____ to mo./yr. _____ Position: _____

22. Is a graduate test (GRE, GMAT, MAT or other) required by your department/program? (see page 5.)

__X__ Yes   _____ No   If yes, which test(s) GRE

Give the date that you took it or plan to take it 10/13/91

Please remember to include the test scores with your application or have them sent to The University of Michigan.

23. What is your native language? Chinese

If your native language is not English, it will be necessary for you to take either the MELAB (Michigan English Language Assessment Battery) or the TOEFL (Test of English as a Foreign Language). Indicate which you plan to take or have taken. (see page 7.)

__X__ TOEFL on (give date) Oct. 1990   If known, list total score 570

_____ MELAB on (give date) _____ If known, list total score _____

24. (Optional)   I hereby authorize (print name) Chao-Lung Wang (UM graduate student Chemistry)   to make inquiries on my behalf during the application process.

Shengkuei Li   李勝奎   Dec. 1, 1992
Signature of Applicant   Date

25. Statement of Purpose

Most admissions and fellowship committees place strong emphasis on this statement. Write in the space provided below and on the following page a concise statement outlining your reasons for graduate study, your professional and research interests, and your career expectations. You may type your Statement of Purpose on a separate sheet. Remember to sign your name and attach it to your application.

(My statement of purpose is included with this application on a

Statement of Purpose continues on back page.

separate sheet of paper.)

I certify that I have read all of the instructions and that I have answered all of the questions completely and truthfully. I understand that misrepresentation of any portion of this application, including supporting credentials and documents, may be cause for cancellation of my admission, financial award or appointment. I also understand that all credentials and documents that I submit become the property of The University of Michigan.

Signature *Shengkuei Li*   李勝奎   Date Dec. 1, 1992
Your signature is required

APPENDIX 5
ANSWERS TO EXERCISES
Chapter One

TRUE/FALSE ACTIVITY

1. **True.** All students from the United States and from other countries must complete some type of written request.
   - Forms must be completed and special documents must be sent.
   - All students must apply for admission and be accepted before they can enroll in university classes.

2. **False.** Every student must apply for himself or herself.
   - The application form must be signed by the student who wants to attend the university.
   - A parent, friend, or educational advisor can assist a student, but each student must submit his or her own application.
   - Some universities even require students to handwrite their answers to the essay part of the application.

3. **True.** Each university has its own application form and makes its own admission decisions. The United States, unlike many countries, has no central processing agency for university applications.

4. **False.** Students can apply to as many universities as they want to each year. Many U.S. students apply to four or five universities, but some apply to six or eight. If you can get good advice from an educational advisor about which universities you should apply to, four or five applications should be enough.

5. **True.** Most colleges and universities charge an application fee between $10 and $65.
   - You pay the money when you send in your application form and other documents.
   - The fees help pay for admission costs—salaries of personnel who work in the office, printing costs of application information, and mailing costs.

6. **False** (but for some colleges this may be **True**). Most students do begin university study in the fall term (August or September). However, many universities permit students to begin in the winter, spring, or summer term.

7. **False.** This is not a requirement for applicants. However, university study is very expensive, and most international students at U.S. universities, especially at the undergraduate level, are self-supported. They or their parents or their government are paying the cost of their U.S. study.

   - Many U.S. students work part-time to help pay for their college costs. Some international students also have part-time jobs at their universities. However, students usually cannot earn enough money from part-time jobs to pay for all their college costs.
   - There are two types of U.S. colleges and universities based on the type of financial funding they receive. At independent or private universities, all students (including international students) pay the same amount of money. At state-supported universities, students who are residents of that state pay one fee, while students who are not residents of that state (including international students) pay a higher fee.

8. **False.** Students do transfer from one university to another, but in order to do so a student must fill in another application form, pay a fee, and have academic records sent to the new university. There is no guarantee that a university will accept a student who wants to transfer from another school. The academic and English language requirements of the two universities may be very different.

9. **True.** Many universities have a special application form for international students. In addition to providing academic background information, international students must provide information about their English proficiency and their financial situation.

10. **True.** Every school has different forms, different requirements, and different dates for sending in the applications.
    - Community colleges usually have the simplest forms and procedures.
    - Some universities have tried to make their forms and information books easy for an international student to read and complete.
    - Some universities even have special admissions offices to handle the special problems of international students.

EXERCISE 1-1

Answers will vary.

EXERCISE 1-2

factors; bachelor's; performance; satisfactory; standardized; full

EXERCISE 1-3

Answers will vary somewhat from student to student. For most students in most countries, the greatest amount of physical and mental effort is needed in gathering financial information for the financial statement and in writing the personal statement or essay. Taking the required tests often produces the most anxiety, and for some students traveling to a distant test site might involve physical and financial difficulty. Although not a difficult task in itself, getting letters of recommendation sent can be the most difficult to achieve successfully if the recommender does not consider the task important.

EXERCISE 1-4

1. c 2. f 3. a 4. d 5. b 6. e

EXERCISE 1-5

Answers will vary.

Chapter Two

EXERCISE 2-1

3. state

4. (A) associate, (B) bachelor's, (M) master's, (D) Ph.D.

5. 1595

6. 4.8 millon bound, 2 million microform

7. 33,776

8. 25,386

9. 114

10. moderately difficult

11. TOEFL, SAT

12. 2/15

13. 138

14. $6,086

15. $2,945

16. 812-855-9086

17. Associate Dean and Director of International Student Services

18. Indiana University Bloomington, Student Services 306, Bloomington, IN 47405 USA

EXERCISE 2-2

1. 1 2. 2 3. 3 4. 5 5. 7
6. 10, 11 7. 9 8. 8 9. 13 10. 12

EXERCISE 2-3

1. His family will pay his expenses.

2. TOEFL and SAT, in September

3. He wants an application form and information about college visits.

4. He wants to study physics or engineering, beginning in Fall 1993.

5. He is completing his junior year of study at a college-preparatory school with evidence of special abilities in physical sciences. He has had classroom instruction in English.

EXERCISE 2-4

Your letter should be well organized and neat, written in good English, and include (1) what you want to study; (2) when you would like to begin study in the United States; (3) what your educational background is; (4) what standard tests you have taken; (5) how you plan to pay for your education; and (6) your name and address.

EXERCISE 2-5

1. 1 2. 1 3. 1 4. 1, 2
5. 2 6. 2 7. 1, 3 8. 3

EXERCISE 2-6

Paragraph 1

1. yes

2. yes

3. no

4. no, not for fall

Paragraph 2

5. yes

6. no

7. It will be difficult because he will be entering halfway through an academic year.

8. on the admissions form

Paragraph 3

9. a research assistant job

10. if his academic records and recommendations confirm that he has been an excellent student

11. Probably a part-time job as a research assistant, but the professor may be referring to a grant or scholarship for the January entrance. Sometimes if a student has a superior background, a department will seek special university grant funds for the student.

Paragraph 4

12. Yes, either the TOEFL or some proficiency test is required of nonnative speakers of English.

13. yes

14. with spoken English

Paragraph 5

15. yes

16. FORTRAN programming and the application of numerical algorithms

Paragraphs 6 and 7

17. yes

18. no, not at this time

19. yes

Chapter Three

EXERCISE 3-1

Future: 1, 3, 6
Past: 2, 4, 5

EXERCISE 3-2

1. has taken

2. will take

3. has taken, will take

EXERCISE 3-3

Answers will vary, but possible answers are:
1. By March 1993 I will have taken the TOEFL.

2. I took the TOEFL on January 5, 1991.

3. I have taken the TOEFL.

EXERCISE 3-4

1. Yes, Jeong Kim should take the GRE subject test in chemistry as well as the regular GRE. Of course, he will also need to take an English proficiency test to show that his English skills are adequate for study in the United States. He might also want to take the TSE (Test of Spoken English) if he is applying for a teaching assistantship.

2. Because Wei Mei Wong wants to study business administration, she should take the GMAT (Graduate Management Admissions Test). The GMAT is given by the same organization that administers the GRE. If Wei Mei wanted to study economics instead of business, she would take the GRE. She also needs to take an English proficiency test like the TOEFL or MELAB.

3. Ali Hamad Al-Kaneeb probably needs neither of these tests, which are used for undergraduate admission to four-year universities. However, even though he has been studying English in the United States, the community college in Chicago will want proof that his English is now adequate to begin academic work in English. He may be asked to submit a TOEFL score, or the community college may have its own English proficiency test, which he has taken. He could probably then submit this score.

EXERCISE 3-5

1. Answers will vary depending on where you are. For example, if you are a Jordanian living in Jordan, contact AMIDEAST in Amman, Jordan. If you are Jordanian living in the United States, contact TOEFL-TSE in Princeton, NJ.

2. Because it takes time to register for the test. It is also possible that the test session will be full, and you will need to wait until the next test date. Also, it takes about two months from the time you take the test for the results to be reported to the university.

3. The bulletin is free.

EXERCISE 3-6

1. 2; 01/17/65 (January 17, 1965)

2. two, the TOEFL and the TSE-A

3. May 9, 1992

4. The TOEFL, US$33; the TSE-A, US$75. She is also buying study materials (Listening to TOEFL) for US$11.

5. 120; Section 4

EXERCISE 3-7

1. March 23, 1992

2. It depends on how efficient the mail service is between her country and the United States. Maria wants it to arrive no later than March 23, 1992. But if she

sends it earlier, she is more certain of a registration place. Seating is limited in most test locations.

3. She will not be registered for the test. ETS must receive her payment *with* the registration form.

4. She was quite complete in filling out her form, but she did not complete Section 10 about how many times she has taken the TOEFL. Fortunately, her registration can be processed without this information.

EXERCISE 3-8

1. 10 2. 3 3. 6 4. 2 5. 11

6. 8 (A student may be admitted to Ohio State, but then not score high enough on Ohio State's test to qualify to take a full academic load. In such a case, a student would take fewer courses than a full academic course *and* be required to take one or more special courses to improve his or her academic writing skills.)

EXERCISE 3-9

1. The graduate program in engineering mechanics may require higher than a 525. A TOEFL score of 500 is the minimum acceptable score. Some departments may require higher scores even to be admitted. Jeong could apply to study at the university's intensive language program or study English in his home country. Then after a few months, he could retake the TOEFL. With a higher score, he might be admitted.

2. The English proficiency requirements of a university are guidelines used by admissions officials. Ahmed will be denied admission with a score of 74 because such a score indicates that he does not have sufficient English to successfully manage both chemistry and English language courses. University officials believe that the academic demands would be too great and that Ahmed would find himself in academic difficulty if he entered the program. His alternatives are similar to Jeong's. He can improve his English skills and then retake the TOEFL.

EXERCISE 3-10

1. 558 verbal, 636 mathematic (see "Typical Profile," paragraph 1)

2. b. extremely

3. a. slightly

4. b. SAT scores

EXERCISE 3-11

1. Both U.S. and international students must take an academic test, the SAT or ACT. International students, whose native language is not English, must also take the TOEFL.

2. two tests: (1) TOEFL, (2) SAT or ACT

3. a. November 1992 (so that scores can reach the university by February 1993)

EXERCISE 3-12

c, e, a, d, f, b

EXERCISE 3-13

1. 4 2. 24 3. 32
4. 9 5. 5 6. 5

EXERCISE 3-14

1. In the previous year—because the scores from the November 3 test will not arrive until five weeks later. If Suki has not taken the SAT yet, she should notify the college(s) that she will be taking the test in November. Her application can be submitted with everything else. ETS will send the college a list of scores from the November test in mid-December.

2. August—because it will take time for the bulletin to reach Jean-Paul and for him to mail in his registration

3. March 6

EXERCISE 3-15

1. **False.** They do not need a test for admission but when they arrive on campus their English is evaluated.

2. **True**

3. **False.** An applicant can take *either* test.

4. **True.** Social Science/Humanities programs often require higher scores than Biological/Physical Sciences/Engineering programs. Psychology is a social science; chemistry is a physical science.

5. **False.** Only score reports directly from the testing service are official.

6. **False.** This university wants official scores sent to the graduate school.

7. **True.** Unless he or she took the MELAB, which contains a writing test, and obtained a score above 85.

8. **True.** Unless an applicant had a very high TOEFL/TWE or MELAB score, admission at this university requires an English test on campus. A very low score on the campus test would suggest that a student has inadequate English for a full academic program load.

9. **True.** This university wants students to take the MELAB because the MELAB provides a score on writ-

ing and speaking. However, strong test scores on the TOEFL-TWE will probably also improve an applicant's chances. If the applicant has taken the TSE and the score is high, he or she should submit those scores as well even though it is not specifically requested to do so. High scores always improve an applicant's chances when accompanied by a good academic record.

10. **False.** The test is used to advise students about English language courses they should take.

11. **True.** At this university international applicants must take another English test in addition to the Academic English Evaluation to show that their English skills are strong enough to teach.

12. **False.** But it does say that high scores *enhance* (improve/help) consideration for support. Financial support is often in the form of a teaching assistantship; therefore the student will need to speak English well to pass the on-campus test given to potential teaching assistants.

Chapter Four

EXERCISE 4-1

2. enrolled 3. equivalent 4. accredited, recognized 5. approximate equivalent 6. semester 7. broken their pattern of enrollment

EXERCISE 4-2

1. undergraduate

2. eighteen

3. no

4. grade 1

5. yes, at the secondary level

6. ages fifteen through eighteen

7. usually four years

8. the main academic subject that a student chooses

9. sciences, social sciences, arts, and humanities

10. one or two other related academic subjects of study

EXERCISE 4-3

1. **False.** It states "at least a bachelor's degree or the equivalent." An applicant must show that he or she has done university work similar to that of an American undergraduate.

2. **True**

3. **True**

4. **False.** It states that a 4.0 GPA is considered the same as a Second Class, Upper Division.

5. **False** and **True.** A student can apply in her or his final year, but previous exam results must show that she or he will probably receive a degree.

EXERCISE 4-4

1. a 2. a 3. a 4. c 5. a 6. b 7. d 8. d 9. e 10. f

EXERCISE 4-5

1. Both 2. B 3. Both

4. B 5. A 6. A 7. Both

EXERCISE 4-6

You probably should not have done this exercise. Instruction 6 tells you *not* to complete the form if your father or mother were born outside the United States. This was an exercise to see how carefully you read and follow instructions.

EXERCISE 4-7

1. graduate 2. yes 3. 25 4. page 3, at the bottom

5. page 1, at the bottom 6. 24 7. 18 8. 22, 23 9. 25, "Statement of Purpose"

EXERCISE 4-8

Please note the additional information provided below the chart.

	A	B	C	D
1.	$10.00	$40.00	$35.00	?
2.	?	No (print or type)	No (print or type)	No (print or type)
3.	No (non-refundable)	No (non-refundable)	No (non-refundable)	? ?
4.	?	?	?	?
5.	Yes	No	Yes	Yes
6.	No	No	No	No
7.	?	Yes	Yes	?
8.	Yes	Yes	No	No
9.	?	?	?	?

4. If you go to a university in person, you can pay cash. But most students apply by mail, and therefore send a check or money order in U.S. dollars. Most forms tell you this. The ones that don't, assume you know this.

6. Often forms will tell you to attach the fee to the top of page one.

7. All universities accept personal checks if they are in U.S. dollars, drawn on a U.S. bank.

8. A is a community college and therefore is for undergraduates.

9. Although universities will not tell you to send the forms airmail, you should!

CHAPTER FIVE

EXERCISE 5-1

1. The last name (Park) and the first name (Jung Hee) are in the wrong order.

2. For "Social Security Number" he has written his student identity number. He should have written "None."

3. He has mixed up the information for "Number," "Street," "City," and "State/Province."

4. He has left "Sex" blank.

5. He has left "Married/Single" blank.

6. He should have written 5/31/68 for "Date of Birth."

7. For "Country of Birth" he has written the town where he was born.

Answers will vary for Figure 5B. Check very carefully that you have provided information correctly.

EXERCISE 5-2

1. You should have checked the box for Business Administration; written **Pre-Accounting** on the line labeled Curriculum name; and filled in these codes: College **A,** Curriculum **03,** Major **501.**

2. You should have filled in the following: in box 1, **MBA;** in box 2, **GRAD BUS ADM** and **same;** and in box 3, **94** for the year and a check in the box marked Fall.

EXERCISE 5-3

1. d 2. e 3. f 4. a 5. b 6. c

EXERCISE 5-4

1. positive
2. positive
3. positive
4. positive
5. negative
6. negative
7. negative
8. positive
9. positive
10. positive

EXERCISE 5-5

Each person will need to write her or his own paragraph about her or his own experiences. The following is a sample paragraph:

I have studied English for eight years. My studies began when I was in middle school and continued into my university work. I consider myself quite competent in reading and writing because the textbooks used in my science classes were in English. In my first two years at university I studied English twice a week. Two of my teachers were native speakers of English, so I have been able to improve my understanding of spoken English. I have always enjoyed English language study and was a member of the English Conversation Club at the university. We sometimes viewed films and then talked about them. I recently had a chance to watch a U.S. news program, CNN News, and I could easily understand most of it. My spoken English is not as strong as my reading and writing, but I have been told by my English teachers that my spoken English is very good.

EXERCISES 5-6, 5-7, and 5-8

Answers will vary.

EXERCISE 5-9

Employment and Practical Experience: Please list in reverse chronological order; attach additional sheet if necessary.			
Name of Employer	Address and Telephone No.	Type of Work	Dates of Employment
Tokyo Insurance Company	2-13-1 Minamisawa, Higashikuruka City, Tokyo, Japan 203 03-3123-9810	secretarial and administrative duties	March 1990 to present
National Motor Corp.	1-2-3 chuou-cho, Meguro-cho Meguro-ku, Tokyo, Japan 152 03-3475-1234	clerical and secretarial duties	March 1988 to March 1990

CHAPTER SIX

EXERCISE 6-1

1. A, B

2. None (But black ink is best because it makes good copies, and your documents will be copied for the committee to read.)

3. None (Some forms give you a lot of space to write; some don't give any space—you must use a separate page. Many universities set limits, such as 500 words or one page. Don't write too much. Admissions officers do not have time to read a lot. That is why many of them are impressed by "concise, well-thought-out essays.")

4. B (C asks you to write on a separate page.)

5. None (But you should!)

6. A asks you for your "plans on completing your education"; C asks you for your "goals."

7. C asks you to answer two of three questions. The others give topics as suggestions.

8. A (But all the universities are interested in these reasons.)

9. B (Other forms use terms such as "achievements," or "accomplishments," which could include prizes. Do mention them, but only if they are very prestigious.)

10. None (A mentions "creative work," which isn't the same as having a job. If your job has been very important to your growth as a person and as a student, then describe how it affected you.)

11. None (For these universities, you must write the personal statement. On some forms the personal statement is optional. Even if it is optional, however, it is a good idea to write one.)

EXERCISES 6-2, 6-3, 6-4, and 6-5

Answers will vary.

CHAPTER SEVEN

EXERCISE 7-1

1. pages 8–22

2. page 9

3. two main types, university (five kinds) and nonuniversity (four kinds)

4. page 28

5. Loans are money you borrow and must pay back later. (Grants are funds given to you which you do not pay back.)

6. page 43

EXERCISE 7-2

1. If Javier shows financial need, he will be eligible for federal financial aid. Financial need will be based on his family's income and possessions.

2. If Geraldo is a permanent resident and his family income is low, he may be an eligible noncitizen.

3. Most legal refugees to the United States are eligible for U.S. federal aid if they have financial need. Desta will be eligible.

EXERCISE 7-3

1. **False.** You can apply for more than one.

2. **True**

3. **False.** At this university they are not the same. But at other universities the names may be interchangeable.

4. **True**

5. **False.** All students can apply for *university* fellowships, but there are other fellowships that have some restrictions.

EXERCISE 7-4

1. February 1

2. February 15

3. March 15

4. April 15

5. April 1

6. early May

EXERCISE 7-5

1. c 2. a 3. a 4. b 5. a

EXERCISE 7-6

1. his family

2. $12,000

3. no

4. the math department of Ohio State

5. a certified bank statement showing that the funds are available

EXERCISE 7-7

The certificate from the Jordan Kuwait Bank is more complete, but it does not show that complete funds are available. It does suggest, however, a regular income of over $100,000.

The certificate from the Bank of Taiwan shows funds, but it is missing all the basic information. It is acceptable, however, if it is accompanied by a signed statement from the parent or sponsor that includes: when the guarantee begins; the applicant's full name; the guarantor's name, address, and relation to applicant; and the amount of support the parent or sponsor will provide the applicant.

EXERCISE 7-8

1. by his or her government

2. $95,000

3. Fees and living expenses increase each year.

4. Yes, it must be documented with a signed letter from the sponsor stating that the specific funds are available from X date to X date, or the student will not be offered admission.

EXERCISE 7-9

Answers will vary.

CHAPTER EIGHT

EXERCISE 8-1

1. B (See "Mailing Instructions.")

2. B (See checklist, 2, and "Mailing Instructions.")

3. B (At least eight—check for application fee, secondary school academic transcripts, national exam results, confidential statement and bank letter, two essays, and letter of recommendation. SAT and TOEFL test scores are sent directly to the university by the Educational Testing Service.)

4. C (See "To enter Boston University as a Transfer.")

5. C (See the note below "Mailing Instructions.")

6. A (See checklist, 4.)

7. B (See checklist, 10.)

8. B (It is better to send what is available if the deadline is near.)

EXERCISE 8-2

1. Kyoto Institute of Technology

2. Kyoto Institute of Technology and Bangkapi Government Secondary School

3. National Chengchi University

4. Bangkapi Government Secondary School

5. National Chengchi University

6. National Chiao Tung University

7. All were considered acceptable by a major U.S. university, but the ones that list courses and grades are most complete.

EXERCISES 8-3 and 8-4

Answers will vary.

EXERCISE 8-5

1. C 2. A 3. B

EXERCISE 8-6

5. NAME LAST	FIRST	MIDDLE/FORMER SURNAME	6. DATE OF BIRTH MO. DAY YR.	7. MALE FEM.
STETLOVOYITCH	EUGENIA		10 12 63	☐ ☑

8. REQUIRED FOR FEDERAL REPORTING BY CIVIL RIGHTS ACT OF 1964 RACE (CHECK ONE)	1. ☐ CAUCASIAN WHITE	3. ☐ ASIAN OR PACIFIC ISLANDER	5. ☐ HISPANIC
	2. ☐ BLACK/NEGRO	4. ☐ AMERICAN INDIAN OR ALASKAN NATIVE	6. ☑ OTHER/FOREIGN STUDENT

9. ARE YOU A CITIZEN OF THE UNITED STATES? YES ☐ NO ☑	IF NO, INDICATE COUNTRY	VISA STATUS	10. BIRTH PLACE COUNTY	STATE	COUNTRY
	USSR	F-1 student	LENINGRAD		USSR

EXERCISE 8-7

1. Answers will vary—probably A.

2. D

3. A, B (Expenses; tuition charges. C mentions the application fee, but that's not part of the contract.)

4. C, D (refusal/cancellation of admission or expulsion; enrollment may be denied)

CHAPTER NINE

EXERCISE 9-1

1. She wants a regular student visa. It is important that she corrects this information because otherwise she may be sent the wrong visa eligibility form.

2. She wants to enter in the fall of 1993 not 1994.

3. Yes.

4. No, it states she will be studying for a master's, but she wants to study for her Ph.D.

5. She does not have a Social Security number yet. Because she does not have one, the university assigned her an identification number. She should use this number in future correspondence with the university.

EXERCISE 9-2

1. Yes, but not to begin academic studies. She is admitted for intensive English language study.

2. She must pass a test given at the end of the program of English language study.

3. It is not stated in the letter.

4. He or she is called a "matriculated" student.

5. Yes, because she has been admitted and is being sent an I-20 for a student visa.

6. It is used to get a visa from the nearest U.S. consulate.

7. It is not clear, however, because the student is being sent a visa, the university may consider her English level nearly adequate. She may need only a few months of English language study prior to entering an academic program.

EXERCISE 9-3

Accepting letter: m, k, c, e, g, d, f, b, a, h, j

Refusing letter: m, k, l, n, g, i, h, j

Credits and Acknowledgments

Grateful acknowledgment is made to the following for permission to reprint material:

Chapter 1

Exercise 1–2, graduate admission requirements for international students (pp. 5–6): Used with permission of University of Houston.

Chapter 3

Exercise 3–2, Junko Kinoshita's form (p. 35): Used with permission of University of Houston; Sanjay Kumar's form (p. 35): Used with permission of Wayne State University, Office of Graduate Admissions.

Exercise 3–3, form (p. 36): Used with permission of Ohio State University.

Exercise 3–8, bulletin excerpt (pp. 43–44): Used with permission of Ohio State University.

Exercise 3–10, profile (pp. 47–48): Used with permission of Bucknell University.

Exercise 3–15, proficiency information (p. 54): Used with permission of University of Michigan.

Chapter 4

Exercise 4–1, excerpt A (p. 58): Used with permission of University of Indiana, Office of Admissions; excerpt B (p. 58): Used with permission of University of Illinois at Urbana-Champaign.

Exercise 4–4, excerpt (p. 61): Used with permission of Indiana University, Office of Admissions.

Figure 4A, excerpt A (p. 63): Used with permission of the Office of International Student Services, Western Michigan University; excerpt B (p. 63): Used with permission of University of Illinois at Urbana-Champaign.

Figure 4B, excerpt A (p. 65): Used with permission of Washtenaw Community College; excerpt B (p. 65): Reprinted by permission of Student Academic Services, Office of the President, University of California; excerpt C (p. 66): Used with permission of Indiana University, Office of Admissions; excerpt D (p. 66): Used with permission of University of Houston.

Chapter 5

Figure 5A, excerpt A (p. 71): Used with permission of University of Houston; excerpt B (p. 71): Used with permission of International Student Services, Western Michigan University.

Figure 5B (p. 72): Reprinted by permission of Student Academic Services, Office of the President, University of California.

Figure 5C, excerpt A (p. 74): Used with permission of Wayne State University, Office of Graduate Admissions; excerpt B (p. 74): Used with permission of Bowling Green State University.

Figure 5D (p. 76): Used with permission of Wayne State University, Office of Graduate Admissions.

Figure 5E, excerpt A (p. 78): Used with permission of Indiana University, Office of Admissions; excerpt B (p. 78): Used with permission of Wayne State University, Office of Graduate Admissions.

Figure 5F, excerpt A (p. 82): Used with permission of Bowling Green State University; excerpt B (p. 82): Used with permission of Indiana University, Office of Admissions.

Figure 5G, excerpts A and C (p. 83): Used with permission of Wayne State University, Office of Graduate Admissions; excerpt B (p. 83): Used with permission of Indiana University, Office of Admissions.

Chapter 6

Figure 6A, excerpt A (p. 90): Used with permission of Bucknell University; excerpt B (p. 90): Used with permission of Boston University; excerpt C (p. 90): Used with permission of Brown University.

Figure 6B, excerpt A (p. 94): Reprinted by permission of Student Academic Services, Office of the President, University of California; excerpt B (p. 94): Used with permission of University of Michigan; excerpt C (p. 94): Used with permission of Denison University.

Chapter 7

Exercise 7–3, excerpts (p. 105): Used with permission of University of Illinois at Urbana-Champaign.

Figure 7C (p. 107): Used with permission of Ohio State University.

Figure 7E (p. 110): Used with permission of University of Michigan.

Chapter 8

Figure 8A (p. 115): Used with permission of Boston University.

Figure 8D, excerpt A (p. 122): Used with permission of Bowling Green State University; excerpt B (p. 122): Used with permission of Indiana University, Office of Admissions; excerpt C (p. 122): Used with permission of University of Houston; excerpt D (p. 122): Used with permission of University of Illinois at Urbana-Champaign.

Figure 8E, excerpt A (p. 125): Used with permission of Eastern Michigan University; excerpt B (p. 125): Reprinted by permission of Student Academic Services, Office of the President, University of California; excerpt C (p. 125): Used with permission of University of Houston.

Figure 8-6, form (p. 126): Used with permission of Bowling Green State University.

Figure 8F, excerpt A (p. 128): Used with permission of Office of International Student Services, Western Michigan University; excerpt B (p. 128): Used with permission of University of Illinois at Urbana-Champaign; excerpt C (p. 128): Used with permission of Bowling Green State University; excerpt D (p. 128): Reprinted by permission of Student Academic Services, Office of the President, University of California.

Chapter 9

Figure 9A (p. 133): Used with permission of University of Michigan.

Figure 9B (p. 134): Used with permission of Wayne State University, Office of Graduate Admissions.

Appendixes

Appendix 4 (pp. 144–146): Used with permission of University of Michigan.

Index

Academic tests
  for graduate applicants
    Graduate Management
      Admissions Test (GMAT),
      53
    Graduate Record Examination
      (GRE) and subject tests, 52
  for undergraduate applicants,
    45-46
    American College Testing
      Program (ACT), 4, 33, 46,
      49, 51
    Scholastic Aptitude Test (SAT),
      4, 33, 46-47, 50-51
Acceptance, writing letters of, 136,
  137
Achievement tests (SAT), 47
Acknowledgment letter, 133
ACT (American College Testing
  Program), 33, 46, 51
  definition of, 4
  information booklet instructions,
    49
  registering for, 46
  student profile section of, 51
Address, importance of accuracy in,
  70
Admission
  delaying your own, 135
  individuality of each decision for,
    135
Admissions offices. See University
  admissions offices
Altered documents, consequences
  of, 120
American College Testing Program
  (ACT), 33, 46, 51

definition of, 4
information booklet instructions,
  49
registering for, 46
student profile section of, 51
Application process
  completion of form
    checklist for, 114, 115
    and future plans, 126
    meeting deadlines for, 126
    signature, 127, 128, 129
    verification of, 132, 133
  form
    applying for, 29
    describing educational
      background on, 79-80
    describing employment
      experience on, 81-83, 85
    importance of reading, 62-64
    instructions on, 58, 73
    mistakes on, 67, 120
    preliminary, 18
  for graduate students, 23-24, 60
  help of English tutor with, 79
  previous applications, 75
  request for materials, 20-21
  time schedule for, 11
  understanding, 7-9
    costs in, 7-8
    difficulties in, 8
    formal language in application
      form, 10
Areas of study, availability of, to
  international students, 62

Bachelor's degree, getting second, 7

CEEB (College Entrance
Examinations Board), 101, 102
Cheerleader, definition of, 4
China International Examinations
Coordination Bureau (CIECB),
41
Civil Rights Act (1964), 75
Class mix, importance of, in
freshman class, 88
Class rank, 79
College Entrance Examinations
Board (CEEB), 101, 102
Community colleges, 141
Conditional acceptance, letter of,
133, 134
Confidential statement of finances,
110
Confirming deposit, 138
Contract, application form as, 127
Cooperation, definition of, 76
Course of study, applying for, 73-74
Credit hours, 79

Dates, standard U.S. style for, 18
Degree names, English translation
of, 120
Disability, definition of, 76

Educational background
describing on application form,
79-80
proof of
academic certificates, 117
transcripts, 116, 118, 119, 120
Educational Testing Service (ETS),
32, 52
ELI-UM (English Language
Institute-University of
Michigan), 41
Employment experience
describing in personal statement,
96
describing on application form,
81-83, 85
English-as-a-second-language class,
37
English Language Institute-University
of Michigan (ELI-UM), 41
English language proficiency tests,
32, 37
and financial awards for graduate
applicants, 53
importance of doing well on, 7

Michigan English Language
Assessment Battery (MELAB),
33, 34, 41, 44, 60
requirements for, 42-44
Test of English as Foreign
Language (TOEFL), 33, 34,
37, 38-41, 44, 45, 47, 55, 60,
77, 78
Test of Spoken English (TSE-A),
33, 38-41, 45
Test of Written English (TWE),
38-41, 44
English language skills, describing
on application form, 77
English verbs, understanding tense
of, 35-36
Ethnicity, indicating, on application
form, 75-76, 77
ETS (Educational Testing Service),
32, 52
Extracurricular activities
definition of, 4
identifying your, 93
importance of, 89

Fellowships, 104
Financial ability
documents showing, 106
confidential statement of
finances, 110
financial certificates, 109
forms and information on, 107
Financial aid package, definition of,
4
Financial assistance/awards
availability of, 100-101
and English language proficiency
tests, 45, 53
for graduate students from
university, 104-105
through private
organizations/businesses, 104
"Financial Planning for Study in
United States," 101, 102
Financial statement, need for, 116
Financial certification
confidential statement of finances,
110
examples of certificates, 109
and I-20 form, 126
providing, 106-108
F-1 student visa, 124

Formal language, on application form, 10
Fraud, checking for, in admission applications, 11
Freshman class, importance of mix of, 88
Funding for U.S. Study: A Guide for Foreign Nationals, 100

Gender, definition of, 76
GMAT (Graduate Management Admissions Test), 53
GPA (grade point average), 79
Graduate admission
    academic tests
        Graduate Management Admissions Test (GMAT), 53
        Graduate Record Examination (GRE) and subject tests, 52, 55
    application for, 5-6, 60
    financial awards and English language proficiency tests, 53
    sample application form, 144-146
Graduate Management Admissions Test (GMAT), 53
Graduate program(s)
    evaluating, 27-28
    getting information about, 23-24
        packet of materials, 23
        professor's reply to student letter, 26, 29
        writing to professor in your field, 24, 25
Graduate Record Examination (GRE), 33, 34, 52, 55
    information booklet, 52
    subject tests, 52

Handicap, definition of, 76
Handwriting, on personal statement, 90
High school grades, importance of, 120

IAP-66 form, 124
International students
    admission requirements for
        graduate applicants, 5-6
        undergraduate applicants, 49
    U.S. universities with most, 142-143

I-20 form, 124, 135
    and financial certification, 126

J-1 exchange visitor visa, 124

Letter of acceptance, writing, 136, 137
Letter of conditional acceptance, 133, 134
Letter of recommendation
    areas covered in, 121
    arranging for, 121-122
    waiver of right to see, 121, 122
    who to ask for, 123
Letter of refusal, writing, 136, 137
Liberal arts, definition of, 4

Mathematical score (SAT), 47
Mathematics, specializing in, 62
Michigan English Language Assessment Battery (MELAB), 33, 34, 44, 60
    registering for, 41
Michigan Test of English Language Proficiency (MTELP). *See* Michigan English Language Assessment Battery (MELAB)
Middle initial (MI), 73
M visa, 124

Name
    importance of accuracy in, 51, 70
    standard form for, in United States, 140
    suffixes with, 73

Official test scores, importance of, 34
Optional, definition of, 76

Peer recommendation, 121
Personal data, giving, 70-71
Personal statement
    handwriting in, 90
    hints for writing, 91-92
    information included in, 88-89
    length of, 90-91
    originality in, 93, 95
    reasons for requiring, 88
    revising, 93-95
    ways in which universities ask for, 90

Peterson's Guide to Graduate Studies, 27
Preliminary application form, 29
  photocopying, 28
  using, 18
Processing fee, and reapplication, 75
Professional programs, applying for, 93
Professor
  graduate student letter to, 24, 25
  reply of, to graduate student letter, 26, 29

Race, defining your, 75-76
RA (research assistant), working for university as, 104
Recommendation, letter of
  areas covered in, 121
  arranging for, 121-122
  waiver of right to see, 121, 122
  who to ask for, 123
Reference books
  Funding for U.S. Study: A Guide for Foreign Nationals, 100
  Peterson's Guide to Graduate Studies, 27
References
  arranging for, 121-122
  waiver of right to see, 121
Refusal, letter of, writing, 136, 137
Request for application material, sample, 20-21
Request for information letter
  sample, 22
  writing, 19
Research assistant (RA), working for university as, 104
Residency
  establishing student, 124
  and in-state tuition, 124, 125

"SAT and Achievement Tests," 46
Scholastic Aptitude Test (SAT), 33, 46-47, 51
  achievement tests, 47
  definition of, 4
  international test dates chart, 50-51
  problems in taking, 51
  registration bulletin, 46, 50
School profile, 79
Semester, definition of, 5
Signature, consequence of, on application form, 127, 129

Social security number
  on application form, 73
  importance of, 70
Statement of purpose, writing, 96
Student government, definition of, 5
Student identification number, 70
Suffixes, 73

"Taking ACT Assessment for Students outside U.S.," 46
"Taking the Achievement Tests," 46-47
"Taking the SAT," 46-47
Teaching assistantship, oral test for, 55
Teaching assistant (TA), working for university as, 104
Technical schools, visa for students of, 124
Telephone calls, making effective, to admissions offices, 97
Testing information
  academic tests
    American College Testing Program (ACT), 33
    Graduate Record Examination (GRE), 33
    Scholastic Aptitude Test (SAT), 33
  English language proficiency tests, 32, 37, 38
    Michigan English Language Assessment Battery (MELAB), 33, 41
    Test of English as Foreign Language (TOEFL), 33, 34, 37, 38-41, 44, 45, 47, 55, 60, 61, 77, 78
    Test of Spoken English (TSE-A), 33, 38-41, 45
    Test of Written English (TWE), 33, 38-41, 44
  general, 32-37
Test of English as Foreign Language (TOEFL), 33, 34, 44, 47, 55, 60, 77
  information bulletin, 38-40
  preparation for, 78
  registering for, 38-41
  sample registration form, 39
  scores on, 37, 45, 61
Test of Spoken English (TSE-A), 33
  and financial assistance, 45

information bulletin, 38-40
registering for, 38-41
sample registration form, 39
Test of Written English (TWE), 33
registering for, 38-41, 44
Test preparation, 37
Test registration
determining which test to take, 36
getting information on, 34
Test scores
allowing time for sending, 32
importance of, 120
importance of official, 34
minimum requirements for, 45
for Scholastic Aptitude Test (SAT)
mathematical, 47
verbal, 47
submitting, 116
TOEFL (Test of English as a Foreign
Language), 33, 34, 44, 47, 55,
60, 77
information bulletin, 38-40
preparation for, 78
registering for, 38-41
sample registration form, 39
scores on, 37, 45, 61
Transcripts, 116, 120
admissions officer's inspection of,
119
mistake in, 120
sample, 118
TSE-A (Test of Spoken English), 33
and financial assistance, 45
information bulletin, 38-40
registering for, 38-41
sample registration form, 39
Tuition waivers, 104
TWE (Test of Written English), 33
registering for, 38-41, 44
Typing, of letters, 29

Undergraduate admission
academic tests for, 45-46
American College Testing
Program (ACT), 4, 33, 46,
49, 51
Scholastic Aptitude Test (SAT),
4, 33, 46-47, 50-51
applying for, in United States, 2-4
to community colleges, 141
United States educational system, 3
United States immigration law, and
financial ability, 116
United States Information Service
(USIS), 14
University (Universities)
choosing, to write to, 14-15
definitions of, 14-15
U.S., with most international
students, 142-143
University admissions offices
making effective telephone calls
to, 97
writing to, 17-19
University profile, 47-48
information included in, 15
samples, 16, 22

Verbal score (SAT), 47
Visa process
and residency, 124, 125
understanding, 124
Vocational programs, applying for,
93
Voluntary, definition of, 76

Wait-listed, 135
Waiver(s)
on reference form, 121, 122
tuition, 104